Sensory Solutions
in the Classroom

of related interest

Simple Stuff to Get Kids Self-Regulating in School
Awesome and In Control Lesson Plans, Worksheets, and Strategies for Learning
Lauren Brukner and Lauren Liebstein Singer
Illustrated by John Smisson
ISBN 978 1 78592 761 4
eISBN 978 1 78450 623 0

Can I tell you about Sensory Processing Difficulties?
A guide for friends, family and professionals
Sue Allen
Illustrated by Mike Medaglia
ISBN 978 1 84905 640 3
eISBN 978 1 78450 137 2

Stay Cool and In Control with the Keep-Calm Guru
Wise Ways for Children to Regulate their Emotions and Senses
Lauren Brukner
Illustrated by Apsley
ISBN 978 1 78592 714 0
eISBN 978 1 78450 300 0

Living Sensationally
Understanding Your Senses
Winnie Dunn
ISBN 978 1 84310 915 0
eISBN 978 1 84642 733 6

SENSORY SOLUTIONS IN THE CLASSROOM

The Teacher's Guide to Fidgeting, Inattention and Restlessness

Monique Thoonsen and **Carmen Lamp**

Foreword by Professor Winnie Dunn

Translated by
Meike Ellens, Monique Thoonsen and Carmen Lamp

Illustrations by Ruud Bijman

Jessica Kingsley Publishers
London and Philadelphia

First edition published in the Netherlands in 2015 by Uitgeverij Pica

First published in the English language in Great Britain in 2022 by Jessica Kingsley Publishers
An Hachette Company

7

A CIP catalogue record for this title is available from the
British Library and the Library of Congress

ISBN 978 1 78592 697 6
eISBN 978 1 78592 698 3

Printed and bound by CPI Group (UK) Ltd, Croydon, CR0 4YY

Jessica Kingsley Publishers' policy is to use papers that are natural, renewable and recyclable
products and made from wood grown in sustainable forests. The logging and manufacturing
processes are expected to conform to the environmental regulations of the country of origin.

Jessica Kingsley Publishers
Carmelite House
50 Victoria Embankment
London EC4Y 0DZ

www.jkp.com

Contents

Part I: Theory: Knowledge Is the Beginning of All Wisdom

   We look at how you process sensory input, follow the process and
   explain what SPI-Glasses are. We explain how 'the bouncer' or the
   'sensory input filter' treats sensory input. We explain what it means
   to be underresponsive and overresponsive and give examples of
   behaviour as a result of this, both inside and outside the classroom.
   We introduce the Fan-model to visualise sensory processing.

   We explain how sensory processing affects your level of alertness. A
   distinction is made between students who may try to influence and
   students who may not try to influence sensory input themselves. We
   provide examples of behaviour as a result of this. We also explain
   how the student can get stressed from being overresponsive and
   what the consequences are for their behaviour in the classroom.

   We practise using the SPI-Glasses. We discuss the eight senses and show
   how they influence behaviour and choices in general. For each sense, we
   give examples of the behaviour of under- and overresponsive students.
   We also show that everyone has their own experience of reality.

Part II: Getting Started: What Can You Do?

   You will receive the instructions for using strategies the right way.
   With the help of a SPI-viewing guide, you can choose an activating
   or calming strategy. We also revisit the Fan-model introduced in
   Chapter 1, which helps the student become aware of their personal
   need for input. We also answer some practical questions.

Part III: What Else Can You Do? Layout, Organization and Didactics

Part IV: The Teacher with SPI-Glasses

Foreword

There was a time a few decades ago when the application of sensory processing knowledge was a new and mysterious area. We knew how the sensory systems worked from neuroscientists. Applied scientists were beginning to experiment with how to take that neuroscience knowledge and use it to conduct assessments and create interventions with children and adults; some of our experiments were useful, and others were not.

As we began to talk about our findings with others, an interesting thing started to happen. People would tell us about their personal life experiences with their own sensory processing. They would tell us about their spouses, neighbours and friends. None of these people had identified conditions we would associate with challenging sensory processing, and yet they were describing similar experiences to people we had studied as a risk group.

As these stories started coming my way, I realized that although what we had learned from children and adults in special groups (e.g. autism, schizophrenia, ADHD) helped us understand sensory processing, these new insights applied to the human experience in general. We were learning about everybody, including ourselves! I began to think about how we could talk about sensory processing as a characteristic rather than a 'deficit' or 'dysfunction'. This realization opened many possibilities beyond our wildest dreams.

As we have all come to understand the importance of sensory processing knowledge for everyone, we have also had to consider new ways to disseminate this information to others. What would parents want to know about how to manage their home and life routines? How could we support families to select community activities that would be satisfying for everyone? How could we partner with teachers and schools to make learning successful?

Monique Thoonsen and Carmen Lamp answered the call to make sensory processing knowledge accessible to teachers and schools in their book, *Sensory Solutions in the Classroom: The Teacher's Guide to Fidgeting, Inattention and Restlessness.* They translated seriously complex material from both neuroscience and applied sciences into everyday explanations that retain accuracy while linking the ideas to the familiar routines at school. Because their tone is conversational, their writing invites educators to imagine ways they can adjust their already effective routines to support students with various responses to sensory events in the classroom. They break their material into manageable parts, so that an educator can learn one part at a time and find pertinent material later as situations arise. They provide many examples so educators can find strategies that match their classroom culture. They give educators another way to understand students' behaviours, therefore expanding the teachers' tools for effectiveness.

Not only is this book a great classroom reference, it is also a great reference for therapists and other professionals because it provides ways to explain sensory processing to others. It is a resource for knowledge in addition to ideas, and so can serve as background support for idea generation and planning. This book creates some common everyday language that increases everyone's ability to be heard and understood. Everyone benefits...and I mean *everyone*. I defy any reader to say they have not seen themselves or someone they know within the explanations, examples and stories the authors provide. When we have more insights about our humanity, we are all better for it.

Thank you, Monique and Carmen, for creating access to this vital information.

Winnie Dunn, PhD, OTR, FAOTA
Distinguished Professor, University of Missouri
Department of Occupational Therapy, USA

Acknowledgements

Monique would like to thank Bart and Son Bram, who have given her all the room needed in all these years to write, write and write some more. During the week, but also evenings, weekends and holidays. She also thanks her mom, dad, Astrid and Vincent, who have been cheering her on all this time. I feel privileged, having all of you around me.

Carmen would like to thank her family: her mom, Marc, Tim and Laura for their ongoing support wherever and whenever she needed it. She also thanks Henk van Atteveld and Belinda van Boxtel, two wonderful educators, who made a difference during her career. Also many thanks to my frister Lynn Ross, who I could call late at night to ask about the English school system.

And okay, we will not go as far as thanking the first *Homo sapiens*, but we would like to thank the people who made our very first Dutch edition possible. Ruud Bijman, for making our words into beautiful accurate drawings, with his unique talent to put a little wink in all of them. Heleen Hess (retired teacher) and Carola Meijer (educational counsellor) for their commitment and feedback that helped us to improve our text. Primary school Het Klimduin in Groet, as they opened their doors for us, so we could observe the lovely teachers and amazing children in their classrooms.

Acknowledgements to the revised English language edition
We would like to thank a number of people for their support in the creation of this English language version of our book. First, Hanneke Meijwaard and Mark Veerman from publishing house Uitgeverij Pica.

Their belief in the possibility of a translation has supported our journey to get it done and we couldn't be happier or prouder.

We would like to thank Emily Badger from Jessica Kingsley Publishers for being enthusiastic about our book and for guiding us through the journey at JKP, answering our many questions and following our suggestions.

Gwen, Kim and Karen, we appreciate the time you spent on the manuscript and sharing your thoughts and insight; they were very helpful. We also thank Marijenne, co-author of the Fan-model, which was done just in time to include in this English language edition.

Most of all we thank Professor Winnie Dunn, for her willingness to write a foreword to our book. We are still grinning and glowing from the words you put on paper for us. Thank you so much!

Introduction

This book is about sensory processing and its impact on learning. The combination of these two things is at the core of this book. It is very important for the teacher to know what happens to a student when they are under- or overresponsive. Everyone can imagine something when they hear the word 'overresponsive'. But many teachers are not aware of the number of students who are underresponsive. As a result, the behaviour of these students is regularly misjudged, leaving the teacher without effective tools to offer. Trying to calm a student that is 'bouncing around' isn't always the solution. Perhaps this student is looking for extra input which they need to be able to focus. In this book, we will find out what happens exactly with under- and overresponsivity.

We wrote this book for primary education because in primary school children are confronted with a system that is adjusted to the 'average child'. The older the child, the more control they'll have in organizing their life. Consequently, their environment and activities will gradually align more with their way of sensory processing. And if a child learns how to deal with under- and overresponsivity at a young age, the more they will benefit later in life.

We provide background information in all chapters, consisting of recognizable situations, examples, theory and research results. The illustrations give you as clear a picture as possible of what sensory processing looks like. We use tables, so you can look things up quickly. You can choose to skip in-depth parts, such as theoretical background and examples of scientific research. To help you adopt the contents of the book as much as possible, we have added assignments and tests. These ensure that you become aware of and experience how sensory processing works. So, it's definitely handy to do these short tests and assignments. But of course, you already know that when you work in education.

Above all, the book is very practical. Because of the recognizable situations, you quickly develop an insight into the process of sensory processing in your students. Part II is intended as a reference work that you can easily consult in the classroom. Our goal is for the student to feel comfortable and safe and to be able to maintain focus during lessons and that they aren't too lethargic or hyper to learn. After reading this book, you can ensure that both you and the student receive the amount of input you need.

Comments

The neurological mechanisms involved in sensory processing are complex. So complex that scientists are still busy discovering exactly how they work. Because this book is an introduction to this subject, we will give you a simplified version of the theory. The theory serves as a basis for understanding what you are going to do. We also use exaggerated examples, because extremes help make our point nice and clear. When you become familiar with these extremes, it will eventually become easier to recognize the many nuances.

There are many reasons for people's behaviour. In this book, we show how sensory processing is connected to behaviour and how it influences learning. That means that we view behaviours in this light. We understand that there are of course other causes of disruptive behaviour.

With most of your students you can start with the information in this book. If you think that a student has a problem for which our solutions are not sufficient, you can get a specialist in the field of sensory processing involved.

The many sources we have consulted over the past (more than 25) years can be found at the back of this book in the Bibliography.

And, lastly, this: for readability, we have chosen to refer to the student as 'they', instead of 'he/she'. We also write 'parent' where we mean 'parent(s) and/or caregiver(s)'. And where we say 'teacher', we also mean other (educational) professionals who work with children.

The following icons are used in this book:

Theoretical background

Scientific research

Assignments and tests

Using the SPI-Glasses

Sections marked by 🖱 are available to download from https://library.jkp.com/redeem using the voucher code RYJGCWX

Part I

THEORY: KNOWLEDGE IS THE BEGINNING OF ALL WISDOM

Sensory processing is a beautiful but complex process. Because it is useful to know how this process works, we start with a theoretical explanation. By knowing the theory, you can better understand the consequences of sensory processing in others and yourself. When you know how sensory input is processed, you understand what the obstacles in this process may look like and what behaviour those obstacles can lead to. Sensory processing impacts the ability to focus and the degree of alertness, and is crucial for being able to learn. It is very important for the student (and of course for you as a teacher) that they can focus as needed, when needed. In this part, we show which disruptive behaviour can be related to disrupted sensory processing. This lays the foundation for being able to support the student in this area. As soon as you are sufficiently capable of recognizing this behaviour, you can start applying the strategies from Part II and Part III.

1

Stimulate Your Sensory Side

What's this chapter about?

In this chapter, we look at how you process sensory input and we explain 'SPI-Glasses (SPI = Sensory Processing of Input)'. These glasses will be used to examine your students' behaviour. We introduce the 'bouncer' and explain how he is involved with sensory input. How he 'grades' that input, and what these grades mean. We show what part of the brain the 'bouncer' resides in and how you can see him as a 'sensory input filter'. We explain what it means to be underresponsive and overresponsive. We present examples of student behaviour you can encounter in class. And finally, we explain how overresponsivity can cause stress.

Let's just start from the beginning: What is sensory processing (SP)?

We will explain the following process in further detail later, but this is the short version: SP means to register information coming from our body and our surroundings through our senses, process it and respond in an appropriate manner.

Sensory processing is one of your body's main tasks. Sensory processing is something everybody does, always and everywhere. You too. Right now. At this moment, your senses are registering all different kinds of input, such as colours, smells and sounds. This input is then transmitted to the brain for processing. The brain gets to work and assesses whether something should be done with the input and, if so, what.

The sensory input is prioritized based on the information it contains. It can be categorized as important, interesting, useful or inconsequential. Depending on the priority assigned to the input, action will be taken.

For example: you pinch your nose, because you think something is smelly (smell sensation), or you turn down the music, because it is too loud (sound sensation).

HOW DOES SENSORY INPUT TRAVEL?

This is the course of events, simplified:

Step 1: Registration

Input is first registered by the senses, for example the ears or the nose. The sound of students talking enters your ear, or the smell of fresh coffee enters your nose. If the sense doesn't work, the process of sensory processing ends here. The input cannot be registered, for example, if you are deaf or have lost your sense of smell.

Step 2: Prioritization

The input is located through the senses into areas of the brain which decide on their importance. Input that is registered a lot and that doesn't require an immediate response is considered of less importance. New input, or input linked to survival, is considered very important. For example, the constant sound (hum) of the computer is not deemed important, while the smell of fresh coffee in the morning is. The consistent smell of your own deodorant is not considered important, so this input will not be passed on. When input is found to be unimportant, the process ends here.

Step 3: Cerebral cortex

If the input is considered sufficiently important, it will be passed on to the cerebral cortex. It isn't until then that you can become aware of the input. You will hear the student or smell the coffee. You're not aware of all the input that is conveyed to the cerebral cortex.

Step 4: Response

After the input has arrived in the cerebral cortex, a response will follow:

- Unconscious response:
  - Stress hormones are issued into the bloodstream in response to a fire alarm.

- A tiny muscle in your ear tenses, to slightly muffle loud sounds.
- Conscious response:
  - You're thinking: Hey, a car!
  - You wipe away a drop that's running down your chin.
  - You walk away from something that smells very bad.

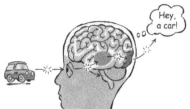

TO DO: YOUR SENSORY INPUT

The best and quickest way to find out what sensory processing is is to see how it works for you. What input are you processing right now? To establish this, we have created a short list of questions. These questions will make you pause and become more aware of your senses. You will see that we're talking about eight senses instead of five. Balance and posture/movement are also registered by specific senses. And sensing the input from tissues, organs, hormonally controlled processes and reflexes is called interoception. These will be explained in Chapter 3. Take a few minutes, grab a pen, and answer the following questions.

Eye	What do you see right now? What kind of lighting is around you; is it artificial or natural?
Ear	What do you hear right now? Is there background noise, and/or are there perhaps noises inside your body?
Nose	What do you smell right now? Do you smell deodorant, or something else?
Mouth	What do you taste right now? Do you taste something you just ate or drank, or something else?

Touch	What do you feel right now? Do you feel your hair, your clothes, your glasses, your shoes?
Balance	Are you balanced? Are you leaning more to the left or to the right?
Movement	Are you moving a little? Are you wiggling your toes, are you blinking?
Interoception	Are you hungry or have you had enough to eat? How fast does your heart beat?

Looking through SPI-Glasses

This assignment should have made you more aware of the fact that sensory input is happening all the time.

You have become someone who can look through (imaginary) SPI-Glasses! SPI stands for Sensory Processing of Input, processing information passed on through the senses (we will explain this in a moment). When wearing

SPI-Glasses, you can see everybody is constantly processing input from outside and inside the body. You know the brain is busy processing all of this input. You are someone who understands that as you are reading this, you can also feel your left ear itching and you're hearing a siren. And that a student is listening to your explanation and in the meantime:

- can hear the wind outside through the open window
- is squinting against the bright sunlight
- sees a fellow student laughing
- feels their left sock slide down a little.

This was a preview of looking through SPI-Glasses. In a later section, we will use these glasses more intensively. This skill is incredibly important for recognizing behaviours linked to sensory processing. We hope you will use your SPI-Glasses very often.

You now know: input enters through our senses and is processed in the brain, where it's decided if actions should follow. So, SP: Sensory Processing. The definition is as follows: SP is the ability to register information from our body and surroundings through the senses, process it and give an appropriate response. Let's take a closer look at that definition, so we can explain the different sections by looking at the processing of sound input.

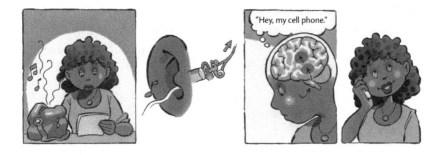

1. Registering information

To get to the act of input processing, whichever sense is being used first has to be able to properly sense the input and register it. If you are completely deaf, for example, you are simply incapable of noticing the sound sensations. If the sense doesn't function properly, because you are hard of hearing or partially sighted, there is still a little sensory processing happening. However, the sense is less capable of properly processing the information and conveying the input to the brain. As such, the brain receives (partially) incorrect information. For example: the ear only conveys some sound sensations, even if the sound is very loud.

> *SP is the ability to register information from our body and surroundings through the senses, process it and give an appropriate response.*

2. Processing input

The second part of the definition is the processing of sensory input, which means sending the signal – the input – through different nerve cells and pathways. The input is considered of high or low importance and processed in that order by the sensory filter in the brain. The input also gets linked to previous experiences with similar input. For this, it is again of importance that everything works accordingly. If the ear can't convey sounds properly, because it can't register them correctly, you can't say afterwards that the brain didn't consider the input of enough importance.

3. An appropriate response

The response must be suited to the situation you are in or the way you are feeling. Examples of appropriate responses are hearing a sound and, depending on the situation, you...

- think: 'What a good song!', because you are in a good mood and want to listen to music
- get up and close the window, because you don't want to hear the neighbour's music while you are having a conversation.

An 'appropriate response' can be different for everyone. For some, an appropriate response to feeling a draught would be to close the window, because they don't like the feeling of the draught. Another, in the same situation, would stay where they are and enjoy the draught, because they're very warm. Previous experiences heavily influence what your response will be. When you associate loud noises with danger you might get scared when a balloon pops.

In this definition, the combination of receiving and processing information and the response to that information is what matters; this should be a fluent process.

The miracle of SP

Clearly, everything our body does is miraculous. But SP is a very special miracle. It's the wonderful cooperation between senses and brain. Through sensory processing, we can register the outside world. By registering input and processing it, we connect to the world, our environments, each other and ourselves. Yet we aren't very aware of it when it's happening.

> *Through sensory processing, we can register the outside world.*

Let's take a moment to look at a situation that's quite common and that takes only a few seconds, to clarify the 'miracle that is SP'.

 You're standing at the kitchen counter and are pouring juice from a carton into a glass. That's one way to describe the situation. But, looking through SPI-Glasses, we notice *much* more is happening:

1. YOU NEED TO STAY BALANCED

While pouring the juice, you are moving your arm and upper body. This means your centre of gravity shifts, and a lot of postural muscles are working to maintain your balance.

2. YOU NEED TO HOLD THE JUICE CARTON

The muscles in your arm and hand sense the weight of the carton and the material it's made of. The fingers then know how hard they need to squeeze the carton to keep a hold on it, so it doesn't fall or get squished.

3. YOU NEED TO POUR THE LIQUID OUT OF THE CARTON

While doing this, you are estimating how much juice is left inside of the carton. You can sense this by the weight of the carton and how the liquid inside of it moves around. Because of this, you know how fast to move the carton, so the liquid comes out at the appropriate speed. If you pour too fast, the liquid can spill over the edge of the glass, or you might overfill the glass so the liquid pours over.

4. YOU NEED TO POUR PRECISELY INTO THE GLASS

The eyes cooperate with your arm muscles to time the movement of your arm and decide on the correct distance between the carton and the glass.

5. YOU NEED TO POUR THE RIGHT AMOUNT OF JUICE INTO THE GLASS

Your eyes are part of the decision-making process to determine the pouring speed, by seeing how much juice is already in the glass. The muscles in your arm slowly lift your arm, so the liquid pours out more easily. Your ears hear the liquid pouring out of the carton, into the glass. The higher-pitched this sound, the more liquid is in the glass.

And then there's the input you aren't aware of, but which is definitely registered and processed by your body in those few seconds it takes to pour a glass of juice:

- the ring you're wearing
- the ticking of the kitchen clock
- the buzzing of the radiator
- the ambient temperature
- the sound of you swallowing
- the blinking of your eyes
- your tongue pressing against the roof of your mouth

- the clothes on your skin:
  - your sleeve is pressing against your wrist
  - your sock has twisted around your ankle
  - your underpants are uncomfortable
  - the collar of your sweater is touching your neck
  - the fabric of your sweater is touching your back
  - your trousers are rubbing the inside of your knee
  - your sweater's fabric is touching your stomach
  - your trouser waistband is a little too tight
  - one leg of your trousers has twisted slightly
  - your other trouser leg has not
- your back is itchy
- your hair is covering your ears
- you can see and feel your glasses
- you can see your nose
- your lips might or might not be chapped
- you can or can't breathe freely through your nose
- the colours and materials of the kitchen counter
- what's on the counter
- the material of your shoe or slipper
- the fly walking across the counter
- the smell of the fresh flowers standing on the kitchen table
- the position of your head
- rumbling in your intestines
- the brightness of the kitchen light
- the material of the floor you're standing on
- what part of your body is leaning against the counter
- the humming of the refrigerator
- people talking in the street outside
- your heart skips a beat
- you feel thirsty
- you look forward to drinking, you love juice and are a bit excited.

You would be overwhelmed if you were aware of every single thing your senses register. You would think twice before doing something as complicated as pouring a drink into a glass. To make sure you can pour a glass of juice without going mad, your brain is working fervently. First, it filters out all information to decide what is important and what isn't. It creates a hierarchy, based on the input's priority.

It is incredibly important that the brain knows which information needs attention, and which can be ignored. The smell of smoke, for example, is important, because it needs to be acted upon – this is vital; but the sound of an aeroplane flying overhead can be ignored.

> *You would be overwhelmed if you were aware of everything your senses register.*

Pleased to meet you: I am the bouncer

We use the bouncer as a metaphor for the sensory filter in the brain. Using this, we will explain how the brain decides which input is important, and as such give a better idea of how input is processed. We take a look at what happens in general with input when you are feeling well, and the brain responds in an appropriate way.

On average, every moment of the day that you are awake, countless different types of sensory input are fighting to be granted access to the cerebral cortex. You can picture this as a large group of people (the input) wanting to get into a trendy nightclub (the cerebral cortex). However, not everybody is allowed in, and most certainly not all at the same time.

The bouncer is working the door and uses a door policy to decide which people (input) get in. He must ensure that the club (cerebral cortex) doesn't stay empty, but it can't get too busy either. People are crowding the door asking to be let in. The bouncer decides who gets in first, and who will be let in after that. Everybody receives their own stamp, signalling their priority.

In this metaphor, getting into the nightclub means that the input reaches the cerebral cortex, which causes a response. The door policy is made up of guidelines: some people are allowed in and some are not. And some are allowed in before others. The bouncer's task is to stamp people accordingly. These stamps show who is allowed in, and in which order.

Who is allowed to go in first? The cerebral cortex's bouncer needs to pay close attention to see if there are people (input) who immediately receive a 'HIGH PRIORITY! PAY ATTENTION TO, NOW! LET IN IMMEDIATELY!' stamp, who get to go in first. These are the *VIPs*, Very Important to Process.

Which input is VIP? Input that signals damage to your body is imminent and input linked to survival should always be VIP. This input warns us of danger, for example:

- you can see and feel a wasp on your hand
- you can smell fire
- you need to go to the toilet.

The next input to be granted access is the *highly interesting* input. This is input that stands out and grabs your attention. This input is very special, for whatever reason.

What is this interesting input? It might be very pleasant input which has your preference, or it could be most unpleasant and needs your attention. Examples are:

- the taste of homemade apple pie
- the smell of wet dog
- the touch of a friend leaning against you.

Note: input from interoception always has at least an 'interesting' stamp and thus takes precedence over many other stimuli.

After this, it is *useful* input's turn to go inside. These are the nightclub's patrons who bring in the most money; the average crowd.

What input is useful? This is input that guarantees we make it through the day okay. It makes sure we adjust to changing situations. Useful input is:

- hearing the sound of the first raindrops falling
- staying balanced while riding your bike
- feeling your hands are still a bit wet after washing them.

Boring input is denied access. They're the ones who are always telling the same stories. Of no interest to a trendy, exclusive club.

What input is boring? This input has been processed so often before; it's not getting any special attention any more. This way, most of the input can be filtered out into the background. It never reaches the cerebral cortex. You are not aware of this input, you don't notice it, so you can continue doing what you were doing. Input such as:

- the glasses on your nose
- the smell of your deodorant
- the way you've been sitting for a while now.

> The bouncer's task is to be a sensory input filter: a filter that lets some input through easily, while other input is refused.

WHERE CAN WE FIND THE BOUNCER (SENSORY INPUT FILTER) EXACTLY?

In different parts of the brain:

In the *formatio reticularis* (reticular formation (RF)), meaning net-like structure

This structure plays an important part in regulating attentiveness. It's like a control room, where important decisions are being made. Functions of the RF to do with senses:

- The RF combines information coming from eyes, ears and balance. Through this, an appropriate response can be decided upon, such as tensing or relaxing muscles to maintain posture and balance.
- The RF decides which sensory information you will be made aware of. It works like a filter for sensory input.
- The RF impacts our sleep–wake rhythms.
- The RF also plays a part in getting used to sensory input which repeats itself and isn't of any importance, while important input causes it to raise an alarm. This way, people who live near train tracks can sleep through the sound of a passing train but will wake up when a siren goes off. This is regulated by the RF.

In the *thalamus*

After sensory input has passed the reticular formation, it reaches the thalamus. The thalamus functions, among other things, as a relay station for sensory input. From the thalamus, input can be relayed to the cerebral cortex, after which you will become aware of it. The thalamus weighs input and decides whether it's important, and to what degree it should be passed on. This goes for all sensory input except smell, which has its own way to the cerebral cortex and doesn't pass the thalamus.

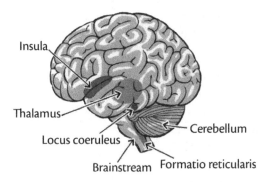

The *neurohormonal system*

Situated in the brain are nuclei that can release certain chemicals. These nuclei influence different areas of the brain and help determine the bouncer's 'door policy'. Examples of these chemicals are:

- norepinephrine, which has an activating effect. It causes more input to be let through (an 'open door policy')
- serotonin, which has a calming effect. It causes less input to be let through (a 'strict door policy').

The *insula*

The insular cortex is the area of the brain where information from the interoceptors, for instance located in internal organs and skin, is processed. The insula processes the sensory input to figure out how we feel. Based on this feeling we undertake action (eat, run away, ask someone out on a date).

Door policy

Based on the door policy, important decisions are made; the bouncer is suited to this task, so usually you can leave this up to him. However, sometimes it can go wrong.

No matter how hot the DJ is, or how beautiful the light show, if the bouncer doesn't let anyone in, the club will go bankrupt. And letting everybody in will cause the club to be too crowded, which people don't like, and neither does the fire department. So, let's see how the bouncer works and how this affects you.

A GOOD BOUNCER GUARANTEES A SUCCESSFUL NIGHT

If the bouncer does his job right, sensory processing will go smoothly. The bouncer makes all the right decisions, and awards everybody the correct stamps. You can function successfully, even though an abundance of input is registered simultaneously. If this is the case, we call this 'neutral' sensory processing. All VIPs, all highly interesting and some useful input is granted access by the bouncer. Some useful and all boring input is denied access. A properly functioning bouncer ensures not too much and not too little input. You can pour the juice without spilling.

How does a person with neutral sensory processing function?

- You don't feel your clothes or your glasses.
- You're not constantly aware of:
  - the buzzing of the computer
  - the ticking of the clock.
- You enjoy many different flavours; you're not afraid to try new things.

 How does a *student with neutral sensory processing* function? The student:

- does not experience classmates discussing something or other background noise as distracting
- isn't bothered by people walking past them and accidentally pushing them or touching them in a different way

- can stay focused working at their table for quite a while, without moving too much
- will raise their hand and ask for permission to go to the toilet, when they feel they need to go.

A STRICT DOOR POLICY CAUSES UNDERRESPONSIVITY

A strict door policy leads to the bouncer dismissing too much input as boring; therefore, this input is hardly noticed. VIP stamps are rarely awarded and barely any input is considered interesting or useful. A lot of input has to stay outside. Input (people) the bouncer has a personal interest in (his own friends, for example) do get noticed and let in. That isn't necessarily input which is considered interesting according to the door policy. The club (cerebral cortex) is pretty empty and there's a crowd waiting outside.

A strict door policy allows less and weaker input through. This causes you to be less aware of certain things; you might not notice a small abrasion, for example. Your skin registers the sensation, but the signal isn't put through to the appropriate receiver. You don't respond as much to information picked up by your senses. This causes you to be less responsive to your environment. You don't receive the right amount of input to 'wake up' your body and stay 'awake'.

When pouring juice, you don't notice the carton is sticky and leaves a sticky residue on your fingers. And if you're talking while pouring, you will pour for just a little too long, because you didn't register the glass was full.

When so little input is let in, we call this *underresponsive*.

Examples of input you might miss when you're underresponsive:

- You don't feel when your clothes are twisted or your trousers are stuck in your sock, and you don't notice your glasses are dirty.
- You aren't bothered by:
  - the computer making strange noises
  - the antique wall clock chiming every half hour.
- You are very flexible when it comes to eating, enjoying strange flavour combinations.

How does an *underresponsive student* function? The student:

- isn't distracted by people discussing something, or other background noise. They might daydream a little, even if the classroom is a bit noisy
- can be a bit rough and clumsy in their movement. They often bump into other people and don't seem to be aware that this might bother them
- has a hard time concentrating. They are a bit sluggish and have difficulty staying alert
- can't stop wriggling because they need to go to the toilet. But they don't understand that the annoying thing they are feeling is an overfilled bladder, which can be solved by going to the toilet.

AN OVERLY EASY-GOING BOUNCER CAN CAUSE OVERRESPONSIVITY

If the bouncer considers all input to be 'Very Important to Process' or highly interesting, all this input is let in with a lot of fuss. The bouncer opens the door wide, too many VIP stamps are awarded, and even useful or boring input gets a VIP stamp. Consequently, it's way too busy and crowded inside. When the cerebral cortex gets this much input to process, you might feel too many sensations and you might feel them too strongly, which can be overwhelming. If too much information is passed on to the cerebral cortex, this information can bother you.

You can't have a conversation and pour a drink at the same time, because it will cause you to miss the glass. You are overly sensitive to the cold carton, and the cat rubbing against your leg makes you jump. It's exhausting to be flooded with so much information. It takes a lot of energy and can even be painful (for example, when being touched or hearing sounds); we call this *brain overload*. This can cause you to respond in an extreme way. When (far) too much input is let through, we call this *overresponsive*.

Examples of input you're aware of when overresponsive:

- You feel your clothes and accessories all day, like twisted socks or glasses.
- You're easily distracted by the sounds of:
  - a computer buzzing
  - a clock ticking.
- You're a picky eater and you prefer eating things you know.

 How does an *overresponsive student* function? The student:

- can't focus when others are talking, they're constantly hearing things they want to respond to
- jumps every time someone touches them, because the sensation of touch is so strong that it startles them
- is very good at sitting still, and they enjoy doing this. As long as they're sitting quietly at their table, other input doesn't bother them as much
- wants to go to the toilet when feeling the slightest urge, because it feels as if they are about to wet themselves.

VARIABLE DOOR POLICY

If the nightclub wants to make a big profit, it's a good idea to have a door policy that considers many different possibilities. A Saturday night would require a stricter door policy than a Wednesday night, because Saturdays are much busier. Because of this, input that's considered 'useful' on Saturday night could just as well be considered 'highly interesting' on a Wednesday. Information priority is variable and influenced by circumstances and the presence of other input.

FEELING POORLY

When you are in good health, it's easier for the bouncer to discern between things that are of importance and things that aren't. Stamps are awarded properly: pain is considered VIP and the sound of your cell phone is highly interesting. The bouncer is more prone to making mistakes when you're tired, sick or stressed, because recovery is prioritized, and more energy is sent there. The bouncer can be too easy-going in these situations, because he doesn't have the energy to make the right choices.

More input is coming in, and it doesn't always have the right stamps. It could occur that an innocent touch gets a VIP stamp and comes through in an exaggerated manner, which causes an agitated response from you. Or maybe the bouncer fails to add a 'useful' stamp to the fact that the floor feels a little slippery. This is inconvenient as it can cause you to slip.

PRECEDENCE

Another door policy is the 'precedence policy'. Certain input that's already been stamped before and is allowed into the club (cerebral cortex) will not be allowed inside in the same capacity, because of the arrival of new input. Imagine a line of people wearing blue sweaters who all get an 'interesting' stamp. Suddenly, a line of people wearing purple sweaters is forming, which catches the bouncer's interest. They will get an 'interesting' stamp now, and the people wearing blue sweaters will receive a 'useful' or 'boring' stamp.

New input can cause old input to receive a different stamp. The input coming from the educational video about sharks might have received an 'interesting' stamp and the student is completely focused on the video. New input announces itself: the bell announcing lunch break rings, and that sound immediately receives an 'interesting' stamp, because the student wants to play outside. The shark video loses importance. At this point, the shark video might be considered 'useful' (the student is watching it half-heartedly, but isn't listening to the audio commentary), or even 'boring' (discussing what he brought for lunch with a friend is more interesting).

This mechanism can be a useful tool to influence sensory processing. For example, if students are distracted and watching a worker outside paving the road, which is highly interesting input, because it is different from what they usually see outside. In this situation, you could use call and response to redirect the students' attention to you, as most students find this fun and interesting.

Safety first: How feeling safe influences sensory processing

How safe you feel affects how sensitive you are to sensory input. The more threatening the environment is (or appears), the more sensitive you are. If you are in danger of falling, you focus on where to find support, not on what someone is saying to you. That's because in order to 'survive' you need as much information as possible about the threatening situation to estimate whether there is sensory input that will cause damage and whether you should respond immediately.

You can experience both physical and emotional danger. For example, there is physical danger when you have to cross a very busy road and there is emotional danger when you are bullied or abused.

When there are (perceived) threats, your body functions in a way that makes sure you are as safe as possible. This involves the body making choices over which you have no conscious control (but which ensure that your survival chances are at a maximum).

During a response to stress you are temporarily not functioning routinely, because you are in survival mode, instead of being able to live and learn. At that moment you cannot expect someone to display the skills they normally have.

This is how it works

It is helpful to know what happens in your body when you yourself or a student react stressed to sensory input. When the brain receives the message that damage may occur to the body, stress mechanisms kick in. A signal of something threatening is, for example, seeing someone approaching fast. But the signal can also consist of sensory input that is too strong, such as a brusque touch, a very loud noise or a bright light. One of the stress mechanisms that comes into effect is that the sensory input filter remains open to all input, because all sensory input may be important for survival. With this information your body decides to fight, flee or freeze in response to the threat.

Imagine a situation where you are face to face with a tiger. It is of vital importance that you can run away, that you hear where the tiger is and that you can estimate how far away it is. You must experience all sensory input to be able to decide upon which action to take.

The mechanism of being hyper-alert and taking action is meant to help you for a short period of time. Being stressed and therefore hyper-alert for a long time is unhealthy. For instance, it's not functional and certainly not healthy when your sensory input filter remains wide open for a long time after only hearing one loud sound. We have to do something that will relax our body, to regain our balance.

People who are overresponsive are 'sharply tuned'. People dealing with chronic stress or trauma therefore respond more defensively than people who do not experience stress.

The three systems and behaviour

To be able to socially interact, which also means being able to ask for help, and to be able to grow, be healthy and respond to danger or life-threatening situations, we have three systems that work together (Porges, 2008, 2011). It is the autonomic nervous system that has the task of adapting the body's actions to a changing environment. It has two types of systems to do this: the parasympathetic – divided into two systems – and the sympathetic system. Each of these three systems can be active and each affects sensory processing differently.

The systems are active in accordance with the requirements of the situation. This usually happens automatically and unconsciously, but we can learn to influence the systems.

The first system

The first system is part of the parasympathetic nervous system. It helps us to be alert and active, but also to rest and recover. We call this the *engage and recovery system.*

Through this system we can process and focus on all sensory stimuli in everyday, normal, safe life. We can focus more or less attention on something. If the engage and recovery system functions well, we can perceive, experience, investigate, communicate and learn. We focus on social sensory input and social resources and can establish and maintain contact and ask for help or comfort.

However, this system is not sufficiently in balance in every person: the underresponsive person does not process all sensory input.

As long as the (autonomic) nervous system experiences the situation as 'sufficiently safe', you can continue to function in this system and there is room for focus, processing, and rest and recovery. With this first system being active, we are able to look for support and comfort when we need it.

The second system

The second system is the sympathetic nervous system. We call this the *stress system*. It controls a fast response to danger. As soon as the situation is no longer sufficiently safe, the second system takes over from the first system. Then we see the survival mechanisms fight, flight or (active) freeze (tensing muscles, to be ready for action) occur.

This second system knows which response creates the best chance of survival and damage control in a stressful or unsafe situation. If our situation is not safe, we limit the processing of sensory input to two things:

- input that is related to the threat
- input that is related to increasing our safety.

For example, we are extra focused on high sounds (screaming for help), on low sounds (from predators) and on movement that signals danger. This sensory input is given priority. We can no longer properly process/understand the sounds of people who talk to us. We focus on our surroundings, to look for sources of help, a flightpath or weapons to defend ourselves.

There are also reactions to sensory input that increase the chance of survival. For example, by laughing, screaming or making primal sounds to release tension, we increase our chance of survival.

The third system

However, if the situation is even more threatening, the *third system* takes over. This system is part of the parasympathetic nervous system, and it activates in life-threatening situations. We call it the *emergency system.*

The survival mechanism involved is the shutdown ('passive freeze'), which causes immobilization (no more movement) and dissociation (no longer perceiving) to save energy and to avoid physical and emotional damage, in order to maximize the chance of survival. When our safety is seriously threatened, we feel paralysed, faint or numb. We disable our basic physical, cognitive and emotional systems and switch 'off' physically to lower the amount of energy our bodily functions need. We may feel we are 'not present' or 'this is not happening to me'. Bowel functioning may stop and we no longer feel or think anything.

Very little sensory input is experienced, only the input that indicates that the complete shutdown (immobilization and dissociation) can be ended. The body must first 'restart' itself before it can function again in a more normal way. You may see behaviour that can be linked to over-responsivity and behaviour that resembles underresponsivity, but that arises from being extremely overwhelmed.

The first system takes over from the second and third systems as soon as the environment is safe(r). The first system is compared to a brake pedal and allows recovery and rest. A brake pedal, because it makes the heart rate go down, among other things. The second system is compared to an accelerator pedal and speed of action, so that we can act quickly to survive. The third system blocks action fast and forcefully, just like an emergency brake. It is harder to go back to the first system from here.

Which behaviours belong with the different systems?

Imagine the following stressful situation: the student will be giving a presentation, which will be graded. There are about 25 students and his teacher looking at him. He has some notes and is using PowerPoint to show pictures and a video. His friend will help him with the PowerPoint presentation. He is very excited, because he will talk about architecture and he loves this subject! But having to present causes him stress too. Will he be able to follow his notes? Are the others going to like it? Will the video work? These are all stress factors that the student tries to keep within bounds. What reactions may the student show?

ENGAGE AND RECOVERY SYSTEM (SYSTEM 1)

The student starts by looking around and smiling to his friends and the teacher. When he discovers there is a problem with the PowerPoint presentation, he walks towards his friend who is helping him set up the presentation. He asks what the problem is and makes a joke. After a while, when he and his friend are not successful in solving the problem, he asks the teacher if they can help. When the PowerPoint presentation is working, he starts his presentation.

Engage and recovery is also being able to:

- relate to how other people feel
- ask for help
- ask someone to comfort you
- make friends
- help others (see that others need help)

- pick up on friendly intentions
- say you are sorry.

FIGHT: STRESS SYSTEM (SYSTEM 2)

The student is about to give his presentation. He tries to stay calm, but expresses his tension by being irritated. He expresses this verbally – not in a nice way – to his friend who is helping him set up the PowerPoint presentation. He may clench his fists and is unable to relax. He starts arguing with his friend and is ordering him around. He picks up the keyboard and almost wants to throw it down. With all these actions he subconsciously tries to keep the tension under control. Eventually, the teacher asks him if he needs to visit the toilet before starting his presentation, and says that they will see to starting his presentation for him. After this he is able to relax and start his presentation.

Fighting is also:

- being irritated
- showing strong emotion (bursting into tears)
- laughing very hard at someone
- showing dominant behaviour
- challenging
- swearing
- clenching fists
- resisting
- not being approachable.

FLIGHT: STRESS SYSTEM (SYSTEM 2)

The student is still in his chair, waiting for his turn. He feels his stomach is clenched, his heart is pounding and when he thinks about the presentation he starts sweating. He goes up to his teacher and tells them he wants to go home, he feels ill. His teacher convinces him to stay and suggests that he may feel better after moving around a bit and eating something. He goes to the toilet and then eats his snack, but keeps fussing. 'I could do it tomorrow. I just don't think I am ready. It would be so much better if I could just prepare some more.' His teacher tells him they thought the presentation was great on the trial run the week before. When it's his turn and he stands in front of the class, the tension abates somewhat and his own passion for the subject overrules most of the stress. Although he has a squeaky voice, he is able to start the presentation.

Fleeing is also:

- refusing
- crying to get out of something
- no longer listening/answering
- not being approachable
- coming up with alternatives
- running away.

FREEZE: STRESS SYSTEM (SYSTEM 2)

The student cannot sit still, he paces back and forth. He is tense, his shoulders hunched, his hands clenched into fists. He doesn't respond to others and is constantly scanning his surroundings. When it's his turn, he marches forward, walking very tensely. He frowns at his classmates. Then he sees his best friend make a funny gesture, something they came up with together. It makes him laugh and he is able to relax a bit. When the presentation doesn't immediately work, he almost starts pacing again. But one look at his friend is enough to make him feel better. When the PowerPoint presentation finally starts up, he breathes a deep sigh of relief and his shoulders relax.

Freeze is also:

- having a clenched jaw
- clawed hands at the ready
- standing at the ready to fight or flee
- constantly checking everything
- not being able to talk
- not being able to listen.

SHUTDOWN: EMERGENCY SYSTEM (SYSTEM 3)

The shutdown is sometimes described as 'freeze'; this is a 'passive freeze' and differs from the (active) 'freeze' described in the above example.

The student walks around, staring vacantly and sits down in his chair, not responding to others. When it is his turn to present, he doesn't seem able to get up from his chair. He produces a blank stare. The teacher and his friend who is helping to set up the PowerPoint presentation have to encourage him multiple times. He finally gets up. He feels lightheaded, as if he is about to pass out. After a short pause, he is able to walk to the front of the classroom. When he discovers there is a problem with the PowerPoint, he sees a way out of having to give the presentation and he starts feeling better. But when that problem is solved with the assistance of the teacher, he feels his legs go weak again. He starts his presentation, but is not able to focus and is chaotic. After a while, he is relieved to see he has passed the halfway point of his presentation. He then becomes more enthusiastic and is able to engage with the other students and the teacher.

Shutdown is also:

- losing oneself in one's own world
- no longer seeing the big picture
- no longer feeling; not thinking about anything
- creating a child's voice or 'falling back' in age
- giving up (after stiffening first, then giving up and releasing all muscle tension)
- fainting.

If someone shows any of the above responses (except for the responses in the engage and recovery system), they are stressed and overresponsive; they need calming down. Strategies and ways to calm them will be discussed in the following chapters.

CONFLICTING TERMS

In trauma counseling, the way in which we can process input is sometimes explained by means of an image of a 'window': the 'window of tolerance' (Siegel, 1999). The window of tolerance cannot be used point-to-point, to explain under- and overresponsivity from sensory integration (SI) theory. The terminology is similar, but the meaning of the terms is not. Also, in this model, underresponsivity in safe situations (the first system) does not have a clear position.

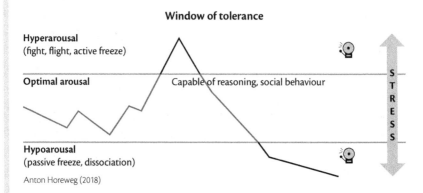

Window of tolerance

Hyperarousal
(fight, flight, active freeze)

Optimal arousal   Capable of reasoning, social behaviour

S
T
R
E
S
S

Hypoarousal
(passive freeze, dissociation)

Anton Horeweg (2018)

Using the window of tolerance model to explain under- and over-responsivity can create confusion. People may associate the terms 'under-arousal' or 'hypo-arousal', with the term 'underresponsive' as it is used in SI-theory. However, this is not the same. The 'shutdown' being illustrated at the bottom of the window of tolerance, together with the terms 'under-arousal' or 'hypo-arousal', is the ultimate survival response (the emergency brake). It is a response to a life-threatening situation. In SI-theory, being underresponsive means that you do not process enough sensory input to be sufficiently alert; it usually has nothing to do with a survival response.

The Fan-model

The Fan-model illustrates the three systems. It is meant as an aid for explaining to your student what systems are active in their body and how they can influence the systems. Although these systems usually function automatically and unconsciously, we can learn to influence them. One of the ways in which you can do this is by using activating and calming strategies. You'll find more on how to use the Fan-model in Chapter 4. First, let's take a look at the model.

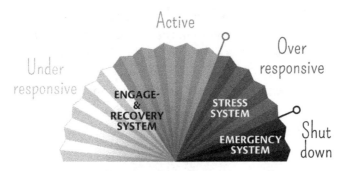

Fan-model by Thoonsen and van der Gaag (2021)

The engage and recovery system is shown on the left-hand side of the fan. The stress system is shown towards the right-hand side of the fan, and the emergency system on the far right.

An underresponsive person needs more activating sensations, so the left-hand part folds together and the centre unfolds more.

An overresponsive person needs calming sensations, folding the right-hand-side and at the same time further unfolding from the centre.

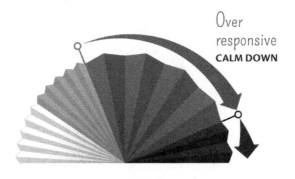

You would like your student to move to a state where they function mostly in the area in the middle of the model. This does not mean they are never in the areas to either side. Rest and recovery happen on the left-hand side. And sometimes you experience stress, which means you are on the right-hand side of the fan. This does not have to be a negative thing. Stress can be a helpful part of life, as long as it is not chronic and debilitating (Parker, 2015).

Active
REGULATION OK

2

Do You Prefer a Double Espresso or a Green Tea?

What's this chapter about?

In this chapter, we start off with a test to see how under- or overresponsive you are. We also explain how sensory processing affects your level of alertness. Through different examples we show behaviour which may be associated with under- and overresponsivity. We differentiate between the behaviour of a student who actively fights the under- or overresponsivity and a student for whom it's something that simply happens to them.

Neutral, underresponsive or overresponsive: What's your situation?

As we've seen in Chapter 1, sensory processing works differently for everyone. One person might not experience enough input and input that is too weak; they are underresponsive. Another might experience too much and too intense input and is overresponsive. Both ways of sensory processing lead to making certain choices, because those choices cause you to receive more or actually less sensory input. Sensory processing can also be mostly well-balanced; we call this 'neutral'. Now let's look at your personal situation. Is everything going smoothly (neutral), are you generally underresponsive or are you more overresponsive? Let's see where you classify on account of the choices you make.

We use the following test to bring you along to the next step in understanding under- and overresponsivity. In this test we look at the choices people make as a result of their sensory processing. Make sure you read the explanation at the end of the chapter, so you can better understand how under- and overresponsivity affect your choices and, as such, your life.

The result, found after the test, gives an indication of the amount of input you are comfortable with. This short test can't conclusively say anything about your under- or overresponsivity.

TO DO: DOUBLE ESPRESSO OR GREEN TEA?

Below are a few example situations. After each example, pick the option that suits you the most.

1. For your birthday, your friend gifts you a dinner at a restaurant of your choice. What will it be?
    a. We'll go to the Italian place around the corner. I will order the spaghetti bolognese (as usual), which is prepared according to a family recipe.
    b. I'll let my friend pick the restaurant.
    c. This is my chance to try that new, trendy Peruvian restaurant. 'Causa' is supposed to be delicious!
2. You really need new sleepwear. What will you buy?
    a. A comfortable sleeping T-shirt with a funny print.
    b. As long as it's shiny and semi-transparent, I'll like it.
    c. A lovely soft and warm flannel pyjama set.
3. While out shopping, you accidentally rip a button off your coat. It falls down a manhole. What do you do?
    a. I keep on walking; I don't mind going with one less button for a short while, with my coat half open.
    b. I walk back two blocks, to a small haberdashery located there. I've seen similar buttons in the window.
    c. I look around to see if I can buy a button somewhere. If I can't, I'll check if I have something at home.
4. When you're at the cinema and the film has ended:
    a. I calmly collect my things and move towards the exit.
    b. I remain seated until most people have left.
    c. I already have my coat on and immediately leave the cinema. I have plans.
5. You prefer to start your day drinking a:
    a. double espresso.
    b. cup of green tea.
    c. coffee, black tea or juice.

Results

Question 1	Answer A	1 point
	Answer B	2 points
	Answer C	3 points
Question 2	Answer A	2 points
	Answer B	3 points
	Answer C	1 point
Question 3	Answer A	3 points
	Answer B	1 point
	Answer C	2 points
Question 4	Answer A	2 points
	Answer B	1 point
	Answer C	3 points
Question 5	Answer A	3 points
	Answer B	1 point
	Answer C	2 points

What type are you?

10–15 points: you are generally *underresponsive*.

6–10 points: you are generally neither under- nor overresponsive. You are *'neutral'*.

5 points or less: you are generally *overresponsive*.

So, what do my answers say about me?

Your answers say something about the amount of input you experience as comfortable. If you prefer to experience neither too much nor too little input, you seem to have a neutral response to input. If you mostly chose the answers that show you prefer a lot of input, you lean towards underresponsivity. If you mostly picked answers with little input, you are probably overresponsive. Besides this, there are other aspects that are brought forward by your choices. We'll clarify this:

What choices does an underresponsive person make?

As an underresponsive person you might look for more and stronger input, because you are lacking this input. See answers 2b and 5a. Surprises and unfamiliar or unexpected input are fine. You don't scare easily, and input doesn't bother you that much. See answer 1c. Because input doesn't come through (strongly) enough, you can be a bit forgetful and planning isn't your strong suit. But this doesn't matter to you; you don't worry easily, are flexible and don't mind doing things last minute. See answer 3a. You like to go exploring and you don't mind if something is a little exciting. You also like variety: diverse input comes through more strongly. See answer 4c.

A warm blanket and a pillow are nice, but if push comes to shove you can sleep anywhere.

What choices does a 'neutral' person make?

If your response to sensory input is neutral, you generally aren't bothered by too much or too little input, because you can filter them appropriately. Because of this, what input is surrounding you is of less importance, and you can handle all input types and quantities. See answers 1b and 2a. Variation isn't necessary, but it is allowed, and you can wait and see what happens in different situations. See answers 3c and 5c. Making plans isn't impacted by the amount of input you can expect from certain surroundings. See answer 4a.

You don't notice the different pillow or sheets when you are staying somewhere else. You can sleep in almost every decent bed.

What choices does an overresponsive person make?

As an overresponsive person, you try to avoid input or you choose more subtle input, because you experience input as too intense, which is unpleasant for you. You are partial to comfort, because comfort means soft and subtle input. See answers 2c and 5b. You like to be in control of the input in your surroundings. You also prefer known input, and you like to organize and plan to ensure this is achieved. You are good at this. This is because it is easier for you to deal with known and expected input. See answers 1a and 3b. You prefer a relatively quiet environment, because there is less input, which lets you recover from overresponsivity. Because of this, you like an environment that isn't too busy, and you enjoy being alone. See answer 4b.

You can't sleep if the sheet beneath you is wrinkled and the duvet cover feels rough. You prefer sleeping at home, because you're used to your own mattress and sheets, and the temperature and darkness of your room.

> **There are very few people who can be perfectly fitted into one category.**

And what if my student can't be pigeonholed?

There are very few people who perfectly fit into one category (which isn't the goal of the test). You might recognize things from both the underresponsive and overresponsive options. How you respond to input partly depends on the circumstances. Students might, for example, be overresponsive more often in November and December, because there are so many exciting things taking place in those months. Of course, teachers might too, because so much must get done during these holiday months. This includes excitement, but also stress, which causes the input filter to be more open.

However, usually you will respond either in a neutral, underresponsive or overresponsive manner. It is good to know this about your student (and yourself); it becomes easier to understand their wiggling and fiddling, because you know the underlying cause of that might be under- or overresponsivity.

Morning rituals exist for a reason

The moment you wake up in the morning, you start processing input. And so you also start regulating under- or overresponsivity. This is an important part of getting ready for work. To do this well, you need to become 'alert'. By alert, we mean how 'awake' you are and how fast you can respond to your environment. The whole day long, you are at a certain level of alertness. That level varies: one moment you're more alert, the next a little less. Every situation requires different levels of alertness; when you are at home on the couch reading a good book, you will need to be less alert than when you are standing in front of the class explaining a complicated equation.

You can build alertness or scale it back by seeking input or avoiding it. A workday's morning ritual is a prime example of this. Let's look at that.

A properly functioning input filter (neutral)

A properly functioning input filter allows the right amount of input to be let through – not too much, and not too little. People whose input filter works properly are generally capable of functioning well without it costing too much energy. From waking up until the start of their work/school day they build the right level of alertness relatively easily: their alarm goes off, they wake up, get out of bed, take a shower, etc. Every action wakes them up a bit more and raises their alertness.

Waking up	
Showering	
Having breakfast	
Riding a bike to work	
Arriving at work	Let's go!

Strict door policy (underresponsive)

If an input filter is too strict, not enough input is let through to become and stay alert. When the input filter stops too much input from coming through, you'll need a lot more and much stronger input than the average person. Otherwise you will stay sleepy and inactive: thus underresponsive.

Waking up	
Showering	
Having breakfast with the radio on	
Riding a bike to work	
Arriving at work	I'm still not fully awake yet.
Drink a double espresso (maybe even two)	
Begin work	Okay, might as well get going. Better get another cup of coffee in a minute.

Open door policy (overresponsive)

Then there's the open door policy, which allows input to come through very intensely and literally act as a wake-up call. This input filter lets too much input through. More input causes you to become *more than* awake and alert. Input leads to being hyper-alert and stressed: overresponsive.

Waking up	
Showering	
Now for a quiet breakfast	
Riding a bike to work, through busy traffic	
Arriving at work	RED ALERT.
First, let's have a cup of green tea	
Begin work	Easy now... Here we go.

Of your students, who is the 'double espresso'?

In the test at the beginning of this chapter and the part about alertness, we spoke about the double espresso and the cup of green tea.

- The double espresso means a lot of caffeine and represents intense input. Caffeine is activating and as a result, more input is let through by the input filter. This is pleasant for the underresponsive student.
- The green tea represents the opposite, it represents mild input. It has a calming effect; less input is let through. This answers the needs of an overresponsive student.

> *Self-regulation can be a reason for wiggling and fiddling behaviour.*

The espresso and tea are metaphors for the behaviours a student might apply to regulate their sensory processing. The behaviours a student exhibits serve the purpose of reaching or preserving the right level of alertness, and as such are *self-regulating* behaviours. You *regulate* your level of alertness your*self* with activating or calming activities. Since it's uncomfortable to experience too much or too little input you want to change this. These behaviours are relatively subconscious, but often effective. There is a mechanism in your body that pushes you into action to restore the input balance. We all do this. All day long. If your attention slips during a meeting, you'll bite your pen, take a sip of your drink or wiggle your leg. You might not have been aware that you were self-regulating when you did these things. However, self-regulation can be a reason for wiggling and fiddling behaviours. Very competent of this student, regulating their own alertness!

Active or passive: It's not a choice

An underresponsive or overresponsive student can go in two directions: they can do something (active) or they can do nothing (passive). Be aware: we don't say the student 'has two choices', because the direction they'll go in isn't really a conscious choice. The behaviours mentioned in the lists aren't calculated either. You could compare it to: if you have an itch, you'll scratch it. Children want to do things right. Behaviours you see as disruptive are, most of the time, those of a student that is trying their hardest to pay attention, trying their best to stay in their chair, to participate. Many students do this by wiggling and fiddling.

Below, we explain what we mean by *active* and *passive*.

ACTIVE

A student who does something about their disrupted input balance is called active. They try to get more or less input through their actions. A student who is underresponsive and is feeling too sluggish to do a drawing assignment at their table might get up from their chair or balance their chair on two legs, for example. They are actively underresponsive. If a student is overresponsive to loud noises and puts their hands over their ears, they are also active. This student acts too, trying to get less input. They are actively overresponsive.

PASSIVE

There is also a group where a disrupted input balance is something that simply happens to them. They don't do anything to regulate their sensory processing themselves; they are passive. When a student is underresponsive and is daydreaming during the instruction, and doesn't do anything about that, they are passively underresponsive. They don't try and find extra input, so they'll know what to do later. They undergo their sluggishness and stay passive. Or the child doesn't protect themselves and doesn't put their hands over their ears if it's very noisy in the classroom. This student is passively overresponsive. They don't do anything to ensure they receive less input.

Active or passive, what does that look like?		
The student is	underresponsive	overresponsive
ACTIVE: takes action, tries to restore input balance	seeks input Characteristics: lively, spontaneous, boisterous/chaotic, asks for a lot of attention, goes on and on and on	avoids input and/or self-soothes Characteristics: structured and decisive, eye for detail, gets tense easily, wants to be in control
PASSIVE: doesn't take action, the situation happens to them	stays sluggish, isn't 'awake' and has a hard time coming into action Characteristics: flexible and sluggish, isn't easily disturbed, misses information, hard to reach	is mostly bothered by input, grumbles, complains and cries Characteristics: sensitive, perceptive, likes quiet, nervous, can suddenly get upset

Following Dunn's model of sensory processing, 1997 (e.g. Dunn, 2013)

The four types of non-neutral behaviours

To practise with your brand new SPI-Glasses, a list of behaviours you can expect with the under- and overresponsive student follows. Of course, this list isn't complete, but it gives an impression of which behaviours might be linked to under- or overresponsivity. We're leaving out the neutral (fifth) type as we don't expect any problems to do with being under- or overresponsive there.

Actively underresponsive (lively, spontaneous, boisterous/chaotic, asks for a lot of attention, goes on and on and on)

This student needs the equivalent of a double espresso to become and stay alert. By moving, the student feels better, and it becomes easier for them to pay attention; their body starts snoozing if they sit still for too long. They will do anything to receive more input, because it's not enjoyable to miss things and not understand what is going on because of that.

They get bored relatively easily, especially in a low-input environment. You cannot tell this student: 'Sit still and pay attention!' because as soon as they sit still, their attention drops, and they *cannot* stay focused.

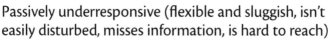

> **You cannot tell this student: 'Sit still and pay attention!'**

They need more input to be able to perform their tasks to a higher standard. They can be extremely active students because of this. When you are wearing your SPI-Glasses, you know: this behaviour works favourably for the student. So, if it's not disturbing anyone, I can leave it like this.

WHAT BEHAVIOURS ARE TYPICAL OF AN ACTIVELY UNDERRESPONSIVE STUDENT?

What might you encounter with a student who is generally underresponsive and takes action, so seeks extra input? They:

- talk a lot
- move a lot and intensely
- chew on anything and everything
- are hyper and very enthusiastic
- walk on their toes instead of their whole foot
- would rather run than walk
- are impulsive
- know little or no fear
- want to touch everybody and everything
- put objects, fingers or clothes in their mouth to suck on, bite, or eat
- stuff their mouth with food
- are enthusiastically looking for excitement and for *more* input
- enjoy being active, they are always moving around
- are constantly doing other things (need a lot of direction)
- get bored easily.

Passively underresponsive (flexible and sluggish, isn't easily disturbed, misses information, is hard to reach)

This student can seem absent, sluggish and disinterested. Their input filter doesn't let enough input in to become and stay alert, so they are often dozing off. This makes it hard to get through to the student and they miss a lot of information. It doesn't have to be the case that the student isn't interested. They just need more and stronger input (remember the double espresso) before it gets through to them. Clearly, this student isn't dreaming all day long. You can expect them to pay better attention after gym class, for example. And because an underresponsive student doesn't get distracted as easily, sometimes they can focus extremely well. This student won't be bothered by things as quickly, and this makes them very flexible. What is less pleasant is that they often miss information and can quickly fall behind.

WHAT BEHAVIOURS ARE TYPICAL OF A PASSIVELY UNDERRESPONSIVE STUDENT?

What can you see in a student who is predominantly underresponsive and passive, so doesn't seek extra input? They:

- don't jump at a loud noise
- are passive, seem uninterested
- are difficult to get into action
- don't respond to their environment; it's harder to make contact with them
- have a lower activity level compared with their peers
- find it difficult to clean up their things
- aren't aware of scrapes or bruises
- are clumsy
- bump into furniture
- throw things on the floor by accident
- trip/fall often
- have a hard time keeping up in gym class compared with their peers
- slouch down
- put their head on their arms or on the table
- aren't good at using objects which require fine motor skills, such as zippers, scissors and pens
- write in letters of varying size
- put either too little or too much pressure on their pencil or pen
- don't respond to being touched

- have difficulty following instructions that contain multiple steps
- don't recognize the needs of others
- don't respect others' personal space
- daydream
- are messy eaters and drinkers
- are very flexible, don't get upset easily
- miss information, need direction.

Actively overresponsive (structured and decisive, eye for detail, gets tense easily, wants to be in control)

This student benefits from the equivalent of a mug of calming green tea. Perhaps you can imagine that the world can feel threatening to this student, filled with too much and too intense input. It makes sense that they try to control as much as they can. If everything goes the way they want it to, the world becomes easier to deal with because they don't get surprised by unknown input. That they try to regulate as much as possible themselves is very competent of them. The student isn't as flexible and can't easily deviate from set rules. The unknown is unpleasant. 'As long as everything goes the way I'm used to, I'll be fine. I will know how to adapt or where I have to brace myself.' This student is very adept at structuring situations; for them, this is a survival strategy. They don't mind being alone; they can enjoy this.

WHAT BEHAVIOURS ARE TYPICAL OF THE ACTIVELY OVERRESPONSIVE STUDENT?
What can you see in a student who is generally overresponsive and who takes action to influence their input balance? They:

- want to decide what happens
- are good at regulating and structuring
- use rituals
- like to retreat, for example in the playground
- 'drift off'; close themselves off
- respond badly to soft or unexpected touches
  – if someone strokes their head or back, they
  might respond in an angry or startled manner
- are overly sensitive to bright light, so even
  indoors they'll want to wear a hat or sunglasses, or they are
  often squinting

- are a picky eater
- stand at either the front or the back of the line
- would rather not play in a busy playground or crowded gym class
- don't want to climb
- pull their hood over their face to withdraw from the world
- wear soft, loose clothing
- fear gym class activities that require them to take their feet off the floor
- don't want to work with glue, finger paint, water, sand and other sticky materials
- are very bossy
- make noises, for example:
  - 'hhmmmm'
  - tongue clicking
  - singing a song, humming
- avoid new situations, changes and challenges
- would rather not participate in group activities
- have difficulty shifting from one situation to another.

Passively overresponsive (sensitive, perceptive, likes quiet, nervous, can suddenly get upset)

This is the student who undergoes too much input and too intense input. This often causes them to be stressed and there is no space for changes in the regular routine. Controlling the environment and activities means controlling the input. But this child isn't good at planning or structuring, which means they often run into unexpected input. In an unfamiliar situation, input can startle them, because it simply happens to them. They also forget their likes and dislikes, so they can't predict what a situation will be like for them. Simply functioning within a known environment and routine already takes a lot of energy out of them. They will grumble and cry relatively often, because the input disturbs them. The student fears new input; they feel unsafe and this can cause extreme responses. The student can also perceive details well.

WHAT BEHAVIOURS ARE TYPICAL OF THE PASSIVELY OVERRESPONSIVE STUDENT?

What can you see in a student who is predominantly overresponsive and passive, so doesn't try to regulate their input balance as much? They:

- notice smells other people don't, which can make them feel sick
- notice details more than other people
- are very aware of their environment, respect others' personal space
- are lively and stressed
- will grumble and be angry more than average
- are easily irritated by, or even get angry about, things others don't understand, for example someone accidentally bumping into them
- have unpredictable explosions of emotion
- have difficulty with activities that require fine motor skills, such as cutting and pasting, because touching materials is a problem
- get startled by and have an extreme response to loud and unexpected sounds
- are easily distracted
- have a strong need for personal space and alone time
- say: 'yes please', because they forget they didn't like that food
- tire faster after demanding or intense activities
- pay attention to their work, colour inside the lines, have neat handwriting
- would rather play with one or two other students than in a large group
- like repetition – the same song or film again
- keep a close eye on everything.

Characteristics of the five types

This table shows the most important characteristics of neutral and under- or overresponsive behaviour. These can help you when you are observing your student and aren't sure which behaviour you are dealing with.

	Neutral	Actively under-responsive	Passively under-responsive	Actively over-responsive	Passively over-responsive
Response to the amount of input	Can deal with the amount of input they encounter *It's not too much and not too little*	Receives too little input or input that is too weak *Needs extra input*	Receives too little input or input that is too weak *Needs extra input*	Receives too much input or input that is too intense *Is bothered by input*	Receives too much input or input that is too intense *Is bothered by input*
Does something or nothing	Usually does what is required or asked for	Seeks extra input	Doesn't seek extra input	Avoids input	Doesn't avoid input
What emotion is present?	Emotions suit the situation	Is (too) enthusiastic and (too) active	Is sluggish/ sleepy and (too) relaxed	Is tense and controlling	Is nervous and tense
Behaviour	Suits the situation, not too active and not too quiet, and relatively flexible	Wants *more*: come on, come on, it's never enough	Is flexible Is indifferent/ absent	Takes care of things Wants to be in control	Grumbles, cries, is withdrawn

The misconception about hyperactive behaviour

We often hear about teachers who classify their students' behaviour as overresponsive behaviour. An instinctive response to this is that one wants to calm the student down, for example by removing sensory input. But you have read just now that the underresponsive active student can portray very lively behaviour because they are looking for *more* input. The student needs this input to feel good and to be able to function better.

By utilizing the characteristics mentioned in the scheme above, it's easy to quickly differentiate between a very lively underresponsive or very lively overresponsive student. Is the student tense? Then they are probably experiencing too much input and calming them down would indeed be the right strategy. Is the student relaxed and (incredibly) enthusiastic? Then they are probably underresponsive and need more input. The student might still need guidance in finding input, so they don't exaggerate and seek too much input, which can cause hyperactivity.

> *Being under- or overresponsive also affects how you feel and how you think about yourself.*

What other behaviour can you see?

Being under- or overresponsive also affects how you feel and how you think about yourself. Most children don't realize they process input differently than others. They only see that they have more difficulty with things than their peers, and they don't understand why. They think they must be doing something wrong, or that they must be stupid.

More characteristics of the under- or overresponsive student can be:

- negative self-image (doesn't understand why things don't work for them that work for others)
- would rather not accept challenges (to prevent failure)
- appears lazy and unmotivated (this can seem to be the case, but the student is trying to avoid activities they think they might not be able to do or handle)
- appears difficult, stubborn and/or manipulative (this can seem to be the case, but the student is just trying to control the amount of input, so they will be able to cope better).

Do I need to do something with all these behaviours?

Are all behaviours that have been mentioned disruptive? Perhaps not as often as you might think. It's nice to be able to put on your SPI-Glasses and consider if the student might be bouncing in their chair to enable themselves to pay better attention. If this is the case, it is in fact competent behaviour. And if it isn't bothering anyone else, you don't need to react to it. When a student doesn't want to come to the school musical, you can talk to them to see if they might have ideas on how to organize this activity so they can come as well: perhaps if they have access to ear protection and sit at the back, close to the exit, they will be comfortable. Perhaps you can't find a solution, and you leave behind a happy student who is relieved that they don't have to go to the loud auditorium, giving them a good chance of getting through the rest of the day without problems.

Know your student

By their choice of clothes, sports, music and hobbies, you can tell a thing or two about a student's response to input: if input generally bothers them or if they seek input. A student who often comes to school wearing sweatpants and with their head covered by their hood might be overresponsive. Wearing certain clothes doesn't only have to be linked to their style preferences but can also be linked to the sensation of the clothes on their skin. Soft and comfortable or rough and prickly, pleasant or itchy.

The student who happily talks about their (numerous) visits to a theme park and what roller coasters they rode while there is more of an input-seeker. The fact that they enjoy theme parks tells you something about how they perceive sounds, lights and movement.

The student who is good at planning and structuring might have a desire to avoid unknown input, perhaps because they are overresponsive.

There are many areas where you can look at a student's preferences and wonder if those preferences might be linked to their level of sensory input sensitivity. Hobbies, room decoration, social contacts and activities, food preferences, music preferences, sports. In the areas where they could make their own decisions, they probably made these decisions because they match their sensory preferences.

Impaired sensory processing in primary school

Why so much attention on the under- and overresponsive student in primary school? Does sensory processing not affect younger or older children? Yes, it definitely does, and attention needs to be paid to that as well. However, in primary school, sensory processing is especially important, because children are functioning within a system that is tuned to 'the average child'. At home, there is a bigger chance that the environment and routine are adjusted to the younger child's capabilities. The parent has known the child for their entire life and therefore knows what they need to feel good. At home, there will be more consideration for the child's preferences, and this is also more possible at home. As a child ages, they get more of a say in their own life. Sports, hobbies, friends, room decoration, higher education and, later in life, their work environment are all areas where they can make more and more of their own decisions. This leads to them being in surroundings where they fit in, where they feel good and that better suit their way of processing sensory input.

These choices aren't as present in primary school. In primary school, a student has relatively little say in how their life is structured. The student has little say in which activities they will be part of, and when and how these will take place. They share the classroom with 20 to 30 other students, must sit still in a chair for elongated periods of time, are not allowed to eat whenever they are hungry, have to go to gym class, play in the playground and come to school meetings. It is impossible for teachers to consider 20 or 30 individual preferences. This means primary school is more likely to be a place where disruptive behaviour linked to impaired sensory processing might show.

And the teacher?

For you as a teacher, it can be useful to know if you are more or less sensitive to sensory input. You respond differently to a group of students if you are overresponsive, and you will allow more commotion if you are underresponsive. Perhaps the test has already provided you with some insight in this matter.

> It is impossible for teachers to take into account 20 or 30 individual preferences.

Imagine a classroom that is in turmoil because the students just heard they are going to do a fun photography project. You stand in front of the class and take in the wave of sounds and movement. The students are all talking at the same time and walking around the room. You enjoy seeing the students this excited, and you take part just as enthusiastically. You walk around and participate in several debates. A colleague might take a completely different approach. She would call for quiet and ask the students to get back in their chairs and be silent. This teacher enjoys the students' enthusiasm about the project as well but prefers discussing it in a calm and structured way. The students each get a turn to tell their ideas, which she then writes down on the interactive whiteboard.

You might end up in a conversation with this same colleague where you don't understand each other at all. Why does that one student bother her, even drive her crazy? You have taught that girl as well, and she's simply an incredibly outgoing, fun girl with a big imagination. Yes, she's very lively and can barely sit still, but that doesn't bother you much. Which one of you is mostly underresponsive and which is overresponsive? This student could be someone who seeks input, and your colleague probably gets overstimulated more easily than you.

A student who is overresponsive might have difficulties with a teacher who enjoys a lot of sensory input. That teacher might talk more and louder, move around more and use a lot of colourful materials. And the other way around, an overresponsive teacher can have a difficult relationship with a student who is often loud and wiggling and fidgeting a lot. It makes sense that a teacher like that wants this student to sit still and be quieter, because that would make it easier for the teacher to function.

With the knowledge from this book you can start making different decisions as a teacher. Wearing the SPI-Glasses you can ensure your student gets *exactly* the input they need – and you do too.

TEST EXPLANATION
Question 1: The restaurant

If you have a desire for more input, that points towards being *underresponsive*. You would sooner choose to be surprised and you enjoy trying new things. You are curious about new experiences.

When you let your friend decide which restaurant to go to, it points towards *neutral* sensory processing and you are less dependent on your environment to have a successful evening. You can have a pleasant evening in a busy restaurant, but also in a quiet restaurant or anything in-between.

If you are *overresponsive,* you prefer to look for input you are already familiar with. You prefer to go the same restaurant over and over, and you always order the same dish so there will be no surprises.

Question 2: New sleepwear

An *underresponsive* person isn't easily bothered by skin sensations, so it doesn't really matter to them what material their clothing is made of. You mostly care about the aesthetics of the clothes and enjoy interesting details such as a shiny or semi-transparent fabric. Whether or not something is comfortable is much less important.

Someone who is *neutral* chooses an average sleeping shirt with a nice print. You don't choose extra input and you also don't go for the extremely comfortable option. If it is reasonably comfortable, you're okay.

Someone who is *overresponsive* is more likely to experience clothes as itchy, prickly and tight, and will choose the most comfortable item. The flannel mentioned in the test is a seamless fit. You prefer over-sized sweaters and jump into sweatpants and house slippers as soon as you get home. No noisy, cold and itchy accessories for you.

Question 3: Losing a button

If you are less aware of input, you're *underresponsive* and aren't as bothered that you lost a coat button. Perhaps you have a button at home, perhaps you don't. And perhaps you'll sew it on soon, and perhaps you won't. Really, you've probably already forgotten about that button as soon as you turn the corner. Until your overresponsive partner points it out to you.

If you process sensory input and respond in a *neutral* way, you deal with situations the moment they arise. You don't plan much, and you don't fail to do things because you forget about them.

Overresponsive people are very perceptive of details. They often know exactly where to find things their roommates cannot find. When their partner or child is looking for their shoes, they'll say: 'They are to the left of the umbrella stand, under the coat rack in the hallway.' While out shopping, they are aware of many things, even things that don't matter at that moment. When losing the button, they connect several facts from their extensive 'database' and remember the little haberdashery. And they *will* go there and buy a button immediately, because they can't deal with a draughty hole in their coat.

Question 4: The end of the film

People who don't strongly experience sensory input, who are *under-responsive*, aren't easily bothered by things. Aside from that, they also often seek extra input. So, when the film has ended, they've already made a new plan. 'Come on, let's go to that fun new bar around the corner, that serves 40 different types of beer!' That the cinema lights haven't been turned on yet, and they must wrestle past people who are still sitting in their chairs, doesn't matter that much to them.

A *neutral* person's response to the end of the film would be to slowly get moving and leave the cinema.

As an *overresponsive* person you would rather wait until the crowd has left the cinema, so you can move towards the exit without any pushing or tripping. You also enjoy listening to the film score accompanying the end credits.

Question 5: Starting your day

The *underresponsive* person needs more and stronger input to get and stay appropriately 'awake'. The caffeine in a double espresso is a handy tool.

If you wake up in a pleasant way and every action 'wakes you up' a bit more, you have a *neutral* response, and a cup of coffee fits perfectly into that routine. You might vary and have a glass of juice or a cup of tea every now and then.

When you are *overresponsive,* you'd rather avoid stimulating beverages such as caffeinated coffee or sugary sodas. Green tea or a sugar-free beverage is a more fitting option. You are already awake enough and will start to feel 'hyper' if you drink (too much) coffee.

3

The First Link: The Eight Senses

What's this chapter about?

In this chapter, we discuss choices you make based on your sensory processing, and we practise using the SPI-Glasses. We cover all the senses and show for each sense how behaviour and choices are influenced by sensory processing.

Choices, choices, choices

Do you have a favourite sweater? Do you wear jewellery around your neck, in your ears, on your fingers and around your wrist, or does even reading this sentence give you the chills? Is there a certain beverage that makes you incredibly happy, because it tastes so good, perhaps feels good as well, leaving a tingling sensation on your tongue, or simply because it quenches your thirst? What choice do you make when you put on music? Do you listen to a live concert of a rap artist or do you prefer a cello concert? Why do you make these choices? It's partly because of the way you process input through your senses. The sweater and jewellery relate to your sense of touch, what you like to feel against your skin. The drink relates to taste and the feeling in your mouth. The music relates to your sense of hearing.

> *Behaviour and choices are influenced by sensory processing.*

How much input can you handle?

Different types of input don't neatly enter one after another; you don't first see flowers through your eyes and then smell them through your nose. This happens simultaneously. As such, input enters through your senses throughout the day, all of which must be registered at the same time. Therefore the senses need to work together. Many things happen at once; you read about this in the example of pouring juice into a glass in Chapter 2. For people who are generally underresponsive this isn't much of a problem. They can function just fine in a situation where their senses are bombarded with an excessive amount of input, at a busy party, for example. This is because they don't process all input. This also means they miss input. For instance, at this party, someone has repeatedly been asking for silence because they want to make an announcement. The underresponsive person doesn't notice this and continues their story about one of their adventures.

People who are overresponsive like to keep things calmer for their senses. They have more difficulties in situations with a lot of input. For example, a busy party will create a lot of input to process. Your ears deal with music and a lot of people talking at once, your eyes take in the environment, partly unfamiliar people and presents, your mouth and nose process a range of different drinks, snacks and smells, and your skin gets touched more often because you are standing and/or sitting relatively close to other people. This also causes your balance to be challenged more, because you have to ensure you can walk to the kitchen or toilet without knocking over someone's drink or tripping over feet or bags. And there was something in the snacks that doesn't agree at all with your stomach, you shouldn't have eaten unfamiliar things. Overresponsive people may prefer not to go to a party, or to not stay as long.

When do you experience the amount of input arriving at your cerebral cortex as enough? Let's use a car journey where you are the one driving as an example. Do you always have the radio on, do you like talking to your passengers? Can you focus sufficiently on driving if this is the case? You're already doing so much!

- Sight: you have to keep an eye on traffic.
- Hearing: you are listening to the sounds of the engine and traffic.
- Smell: you smell the washer fluid.
- Taste: you are chewing on a sweet.

- Touch: you are dealing with the temperature in the car.
- Movement: you are controlling the pressure you are putting on the accelerator pedal, brake and clutch.
- Balance: you take a quick look over your shoulder.
- Interoception: you are peckish, your stomach is asking for a little something to eat.

What choices do you make in the car? If you do have the radio turned on, do you leave it on when you're driving in a strange city and you've almost reached your destination? Or do you turn the radio off, because you need to be able to focus extra hard on certain input to find the right address? And does the same go for conversations with your passenger? Do you end the conversation when you've almost reached the unfamiliar destination? The overresponsive person will indeed turn off the radio and end the conversation. The person who is mostly underresponsive isn't as bothered by all this input, and will most likely leave the radio on and continue the conversation. They can handle more input at once, because not all input reaches the cerebral cortex.

TO DO: HELLO! IN THREE SECONDS

Imagine the following situation: you are standing in the doorway, you hear the first school bell ring, the first student is standing in front of you, you shake their hand to welcome them and they shake your hand. Write below, after each sense, what input comes in through that sense in these few seconds.

Sound

_____

_____

_____

_____

Movement and posture

_____

_____

_____

_____

Sight

_____

_____

_____

_____

Touch

_____

_____

_____

_____

Balance

_____

_____

_____

_____

Taste

_____

_____

_____

_____

Smell

_____

_____

_____

_____

Interoception

_____

_____

_____

_____

This is what we noticed in our senses:

Sound

- You hear voices: high-pitched voices, low-pitched voices.
- You register words: your name, for example.
- You hear sounds coming in from outside.
- The student wishes you a good morning.
- A chair is put on the floor.

Movement and posture

- The student shakes your hand.
- You feel if the handshake is firm or weak.
- You are standing; your postural muscles are working to keep you balanced.
- You bend your knees slightly so you can look the student in the eyes.
- You move your head to look around.

Sight

- You see and hear the student; you register what they are wearing.
- You see how they styled their hair and what their face looks like (for example, red from the cold, healthy).
- You see their facial expression; they're smiling at you.
- You see a drawing has fallen down from the wall.
- You see the lights in the hallway.

Touch

- You feel the student's hand (the hand is warm or cold, wet or dry).
- You feel the fingers being pressed together and your ring getting trapped for a second.
- You feel the fabric of the student's sweater brushing against your fingers.
- You feel your glasses sliding down your nose (from bending over).
- Your mouth is dry.

Balance

- You feel how fast you are bending over.
- You move one foot to stay balanced.
- Postural muscles are tensing to keep you balanced.
- Your head moves to keep your eyes and head aligned, to help your balance.

Taste

- You taste the tea you were drinking before, with just a little too much sugar.

Smell

- You smell the student's wet clothes.
- You smell something like perfume or fabric softener on the student; the smell is familiar, you like it.

Interoception

- You feel you are still thirsty.
- Your heart is pounding with excitement; this is going to be a great day!

That is a lot of input for a short couple of seconds, and we could mention much more. It shows once more how much input is out there and of how much of that input we become aware. *And* how much more input there is that gets ignored.

Your own unique reality

The senses cooperate with the brain so you can become aware of what is happening around you and in your own body. You experience the world around you and receive information about your body through your senses. You use them to perceive a small part of reality. Take the buzzing of the computer: that buzz is always there when the computer is turned on. These sound waves are in the air constantly and are constantly being received by the ear. Yet, most of the time, you don't hear them. It isn't until you turn off the computer that the silence makes you aware of the fact that you've been perceiving this buzzing all this time, without consciously realizing it. So: sometimes you do consciously experience input, and sometimes you don't. At those moments, it might seem as though not all input has been transmitted to your cerebral cortex, but this isn't the case. All input has been registered by the sense and transmitted to the brain, but it was marked as boring/unimportant by the sensory input filter, and as such has not been brought to your awareness. These decisions are made in the input filter without you knowing it. It's not until someone points out the buzzing to you, or it disappears suddenly, that you become conscious of it. Therefore, we can say that sensory processing affects how you experience reality. Before, it seemed as though the world was made up of a not-buzzing computer. Afterwards, it turned out there was buzzing in the world, but you just weren't aware of it.

This shows how your reality is influenced by sensory processing. So this is one of the reasons that you have certain preferences: one person might love sweet, another prefers savoury. This has nothing to do with the flavours in the food, because these are the same for everyone and everyone registers them as such through the taste sensors. What matters is your perception of reality (in this case: the taste of the food). The input registered by the sense isn't necessarily the same input that arrives at the cerebral cortex. Between registering and becoming conscious of input lies a long and winding road, with a doorman and stamps, i.e. the input filter. On this road, true reality is changed into your own personal reality. Your reality is created by *how* you see, *how* hungry you are, *how* you smell. This has to do with how your sensory processing takes place. This means that your awareness is an interpretation of reality. And *that* is incredibly important knowledge! You can't assume someone else experiences the outside temperature the same way you do, perceives a sound at the same volume, enjoys the spiciness of the hot sauce the way you do, or experiences the itching of a knitted sweater as just as annoying as you do. 'Come ride the roller coaster with me, it's fun!' is a strange thing to say, when looking at it like this. You cannot know what another person might think is fun, pleasant, beautiful or comfortable.

> *Your reality is created by how you see, how hungry you are, how you smell.*

So, let's see what senses we are talking about and how they can determine our behaviour. By discussing each sense individually, you will get a good impression of the influence sensory processing has on behaviour.

I thought there were only five senses?

In school, we learned that there are five senses; the senses named by Aristotle in classic antiquity. However, experts have come to disagree about the idea that these are all the senses. Depending on what definition you use, different numbers are mentioned. Within the field of sensory processing, we recognize that there are eight senses. Eight? Yes, Aristotle's: sight, hearing, smell, touch and taste. And then three lesser known ones: balance and posture/movement (these two senses are also called *the vestibular system* and *proprioception*). Finally, interoception lets you sense feelings within your body, for instance temperature, heartbeat, thirst, muscle tension and emotions.

We will discuss all eight senses one by one. We will tell you:

- the theory behind how the sense functions
- how the sense (working with the input filter, naturally) directs our life

- a little bit of scientific information about how the sense influences our behaviour
- how you encounter the sense in general at school
- how the underresponsive student experiences input through this sense
- how the overresponsive student experiences input through this sense.

Sensitivity per sense

For all the eight senses, the input filter makes individual decisions on *if* and how strongly the input will be transmitted. It can happen that the input filter treats all sounds as VIP, which can cause overresponsivity to sounds. Simultaneously, the input filter might consider input from muscles and joints to be 'boring', which can lead to you not experiencing enough movement input. This means you are overresponsive to sounds, and underresponsive to movement. There are many different possible combinations of underresponsive, neutral and overresponsive. This would be too much to discuss in this book.

HEARING
Sound waves arrive at the cochlea through the outer, middle and inner ear. The cochlea is a small, spiral-shaped tube filled with fluid. In the cochlea, sound waves are transformed into an electric signal, which is sent to the brain through the acoustic nerve.

How does hearing direct our life?

An example is your choice of a place to live. Living in a rural area, you will be exposed to fewer sounds than when you are living in a busy city. Some people enjoy sounds and are uncomfortable when surrounded by silence. Others would rather retreat occasionally, to escape the mishmash of sounds, and they prefer living in a quiet environment. Indoors, people also make different decisions regarding sound: whether to turn on the radio or TV, and at higher or lower volume.

In severe cases, sounds can hurt, which can cause a fight, flight or freeze response.

HEARING AND SCIENCE

Music is known for its capability to help us regulate our emotions, influencing our mood and changing our physical state of being by quickening or slowing down our heart rate (Saarikallio, 2011).

Emily Anthes writes in *Psychology Today* (2010): 'Shoppers make more impulsive purchases when they're overstimulated. Loud volume leads to sensory overload, which weakens self-control.'

Hearing in school

Every school environment has a wide array of sounds: there are a lot of kids in one space, teachers are providing instructions, there are sounds in the auditorium during assemblies. And then there are the many voices outside during recess, the chaos in the changing rooms and the exuberance during PE. There aren't many places in a school that are consistently quiet during the day, barring a few designated quiet zones.

The acoustics in a classroom change depending on where you are in the room. This can cause a teacher to think a student isn't paying attention, while actually the student is incapable of following the instructions as they can't hear them (the instructions) or you. Performing regular checks to ensure everybody can hear you properly is never time wasted.

From our 35th year of life, we are unable to hear the highest pitched sounds. The older teacher hears sounds differently than the younger students.

The underresponsive student

When a student, despite proper acoustics, doesn't hear enough sounds, they don't always respond when being called and they can miss (part of) the verbal instructions. The underresponsive student will therefore ask you to repeat words more often: 'What?' 'Huh?' 'What did you say?' They might seem deaf, but they aren't. The underresponsive student also continues talking when a bell rings or when something hits the floor loudly. They simply don't notice these sounds and are surprised when others are distracted by them.

The overresponsive student

The student who can't properly isolate themselves from sounds can have a hard time working independently. When a student is overly sensitive to sounds, they are distracted by the buzzing of the smart board, the ticking of the clock or a group of students discussing something on the other side of the classroom. It takes more energy from this student to perform their task satisfactorily, because their cerebral cortex is receiving more input.

A student might also be bothered by the sirens of an ambulance or fire engine long after the vehicle has passed. Their body has released a lot more adrenaline due to this loud noise than the body of a student of average sensitivity. The overresponsive student needs more time to recover from this shock.

When working together in groups, the overresponsive student can have difficulty registering and interpreting different voices, because they cannot distinguish well between sounds that they hear at the same time.

SIGHT

The eye transmits information about your surroundings to the brain, which results in your ability to see things. Light enters the eye through the pupil, the black area in the centre of the eye, and arrives at the cornea. From the cornea, light signals are transmitted to the cerebral cortex 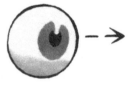 through photoreceptors. Once there, the signals become an image. The eye itself doesn't 'see'; seeing takes place in the cerebral cortex.

How does sight direct our life?

Light can be used to create a certain mood. When you are in an environment lit by fluorescent lights, you will feel differently than in an environment lit by dimmed lights or candlelight. A day with little sunshine because of a dense layer of cloud feels different than a bright and sunny day. Too much light can be uncomfortable, which may cause you to put on sunglasses or pull down the blinds.

SIGHT AND SCIENCE

Light therapy seems to have a positive effect on people suffering from depression, whether the depression is caused by light deficiency or not, at least in addition to medication. And in some cases, light therapy could make medication obsolete (Golden *et al.*, 2005).

Studies have been conducted to research the effect of overly decorated classrooms. A small study showed that a heavily decorated space had negative effects on learning results. Children received six lessons and were tested on how much they remembered. The control group, who had had lessons in a moderately decorated classroom, answered 55 percent of the answers correctly, while the group in the heavily decorated classroom gave 42 percent correct answers. Students in the heavily decorated classroom were less focused on their task and more easily distracted (Fisher, Godwin and Seltman, 2014).

 Sight in school

The walls in the classroom are covered in information about reading and maths, drawings, photographs, posters, etc. This is cosy and is supposed to convey information. It can be nice to slip into a daydream, staring at the busy walls. The student can picture themselves in an alphabet paradise, where every letter has a different flavour, or in a mathematics playground, where numbers are meant to be climbed on and slid down off. But, as you have read above, all this information can also be a distraction.

Another important thing is the lighting in the classroom. Perhaps some students are sitting in full sunlight while the bright light bothers them.

Chapter 8 discusses decoration of the classroom and how it affects students in more detail.

The underresponsive student

The student who needs more input to function properly will not get to work easily when their view is a boring, empty wall. The student who is visually underresponsive works more efficiently when they receive more visual information, for example with books crowded with content that screams off the

pages – alternating between text, text boxes, images, cartoons, etc. They will need brighter lights to be able to focus. The screen's brightness settings will be on 100 percent.

The overresponsive student

The student who is visually overresponsive might be bothered by bright lights, and heavily adorned walls will distract them more than average. When this student is sitting next to a window, or has a view of the corridor, they will be more easily distracted when they can see movement happening. The visually overresponsive student can have a hard time finding the right material or right image in a busy background. It's difficult for them to find the right instructions in a jam-packed book that offers information in many different ways (text, text boxes, images, cartoons, etc).

MOVEMENT

The movement sense (proprioception) registers input through receptors in our muscles, tendons and ligaments. This sense makes you feel the position of your joints and ensures you feel movements. Without having to look, you can feel exactly where and in what position your body parts are and how you are moving. This enables  you to negotiate kerbs, without having to look at your legs and the kerb, and allows you to know without looking at your hand whether your fingers are extended or flexed. Movement works together with touch, balance and sight. You need movement sense, among other things, to keep body parts in a specific position for a prolonged period. The muscles tense or relax in order to maintain a certain position. This happens mostly subconsciously.

How does movement direct our life?

You are unaware of how much you can move on 'autopilot' because you use the movement sense, until something changes. When a chair is lower than you expected, you will 'fall' the last few centimetres to the seat.

And when you step into an unfamiliar car, you might bump your head because the door frame is lower than you're used to.

> *In a familiar situation, the receptors know exactly where and when to stop a movement.*

In a familiar situation, the receptors know exactly where and when to stop a movement. In a new situation, however, you will need to use sight and sometimes touch to calibrate the movements, for example when you walk up a set of stairs that has very different dimensions regarding step length and height than you're used to. In our daily life, we use this sense often; it allows us to move around without thought.

MOVEMENT AND SCIENCE
Steps vary in height and depth, but building standards for stairs do exist: the height between two steps is called the riser, and the depth the tread. A decently climbable set of stairs follows the following formula: (2 x riser) + (1 x tread) = 590 mm. In this calculation, 590 is the so-called step modulus. This formula for calculating the climbability of stairs is called the 'tripping formula' (De Vree, n.d.).

Ankle injuries are the second most common sports injury in the Netherlands (Veiligheid.nl, n.d.). One study set out to see if a training programme would influence reoccurrence of ankle injuries. Results showed that people who had followed a training programme that focused on movement and balance sense were far less likely to injure their ankle again. This research showed a decrease of 35 percent (Hupperets, Verhagen and van Mechelen, 2009).

 Movement in school
When kids start a new class, they will be a bit clumsy during the first days or weeks when it comes to walking around, sitting down, grabbing things from the cupboard, etc. However, once they're used to where all the desks and chairs are and how high they are, how drawers open and close and where everything needs to be put away, their movements will become more fluent and faster, and they won't bump into things as often anymore. Their receptors have calibrated to how small, big and fast movements can or should be.

The underresponsive student

A student who is underresponsive when it comes to movement doesn't feel their body as much, and will have more difficulty retaining the right position. This can cause them to 'slouch' or to move a lot. Moving allows them to collect information in their body and can make them feel things better. They can also be much rougher in their movements, for example when playing tag or during PE.

They will be less sensitive to how hard they bump into something or someone. They will probably bump into things or people more often, because they don't feel their movement as well, and aren't as aware of their position in space in relation to others. It's easier for them to trip, because they don't have sufficient awareness of where their feet are in relation to their environment. Movements are generally less coordinated. This can also impact their writing skills: because they don't fully feel what they are doing, they might not push their pen down hard enough, or might push it too hard.

The overresponsive student

The student who is overresponsive might be more comfortable staying put in their seat. This limits the input entering their body through the movement sense. Even when they are sitting still, they can feel their muscles and joints, which can be incredibly distracting. The student can have stiff posture and avoid movement, because they experience all movement very intensely in their muscles and joints. They have difficulty with other people moving them around (for example, taking their hand to lead them somewhere).

TOUCH

The skin contains receptors that allow you to feel. Different receptors (as there are three different touch receptors) register touch (touch receptors), temperature (thermoreceptors) and pain (nociceptors).

Some areas of our skin have many touch receptors, like the fingertips and lips. Other areas, like your back, have significantly fewer; consequently, those areas are less sensitive. Light touch is detected by different receptors than firm touch. Signals of firm touch have precedence over signals that are being transmitted by pain receptors. Therefore, firmly rubbing a painful spot can help alleviate pain.

How does touch direct our life?

People can calm down when someone else comforts them by rubbing their back or holding their hand. Skin-to-skin contact can have a calming and bonding effect. Touching each other is a way to feel socially connected as well.

Choices you make regarding the fabric of your clothing, type of towels and bedding influence your comfort. This also applies to materials your furniture is made of, and whether you have cushions on your couch. The flooring in your house will influence your choice to go barefoot, or wear socks or slippers.

When you lift a mug or glass, the heat you feel will tell you the approximate temperature of your tea or coffee and whether you can drink it.

TOUCH AND SCIENCE

Failure to meet tactile and stimulation needs produced poor health outcomes and marked developmental delays in infants and children (Frank *et al.*, 1996).

A meta-analysis showed that even single applications of massage therapy reduced patient state anxiety, blood pressure and heart-rate, but not depressive mood. However, when multiple applications of massage therapy were used, depression was found to be significantly reduced (Moyer, Rounds and Hannum, 2004).

 Touch in school

At the start of the school day, when going outside or changing classrooms, many students are in the corridor at the same time. This increases the chance of being touched. Not everyone enjoys this.

During PE, some students will prefer hard balls and others soft balls. And some might want to exercise barefoot, while others will want to wear trainers at all times.

The underresponsive student

The student who is underresponsive when it comes to touch will cross other people's boundaries faster. This is because they are looking for extra sensory information through touch. They do this by coming too close, because they are not aware of what an appropriate distance is. During PE, they might be a bit rougher. When the game requires touching each other, helping each other with certain movements or involves other ways of cooperating, this student might be a bit rough when handling someone else. This student will also be fidgeting a lot, with themselves and materials, but sometimes also with fellow students.

The overresponsive student

The student who is overresponsive when it comes to touch can respond in an irritated or angry manner to unexpected touch. The student might choose to be the first or last to get into the corridor, so they don't have to push and shove as much. Preference for the end of the line makes sense when you prefer not to be touched unexpectedly. When you are sitting at a desk in the classroom that has lots of students walking by, the chances of being touched (unexpectedly) are higher. This is stressful for the overresponsive student.

The overresponsive student can complain about socks, shoes and labels, because they feel them all day long. When they have been playing with sand, they would rather shower before moving on to another activity, because they feel every grain of sand on their skin.

BALANCE

In the inner ear we find the vestibular system. This organ contains sensory cells which are sensitive to acceleration/deceleration and rotation. These cells are connected to a nerve which transmits the signals to the brain.

Through the vestibular system, you become aware of gravity. It helps the body orientate on the environment and literally to stay balanced. The vestibular system collects information on movement and balance; it registers how we rotate and how fast or slow we are moving. The vestibular system signals whether we are accelerating or decelerating. This allows us to learn about moving around in the space surrounding us and helps us develop a sense of depth.

The vestibular system influences our postural muscles and eye muscles. It can influence the position of the eyes and the body in order to put or keep these in the correct position. This involves co-operating with other senses, such as movement, touch and sight.

How does balance direct our life?

How well you process input in your vestibular system affects how you move around. Can you ride a bike with two heavy bags of groceries, holding flowers in your hand, and with a kid on the back of your bike? Does climbing a high ladder to clean the gutters pose no problem for you, or would you rather have someone else do this?

The choice to play sports and which sports to play can also be linked to the vestibular system. Sports like parachuting, racing, ballet, skiing and mountain biking cause a high input to your vestibular system. These sports are more likely to be chosen by underresponsive people.

BALANCE AND SCIENCE

Schilling and colleagues (2003) studied the effects of using a therapy ball in class, which stimulates the vestibular system and movement sensors. They saw that students with ADHD, when sitting on a therapy ball, were more likely to stay at their desk and their writing became more legible.

After a brain haemorrhage, approximately 10 percent of patients end up with Pusher syndrome (Pedersen *et al.*, 1996), which causes the awareness of their posture in relation to gravity to change. When these patients are sitting down or standing up, they'll push themselves towards their affected side, which causes them to fall over. They have a deviating sense of 'upright'; the information coming from their vestibular system is no longer correct. Because the processing of visual input remains the same, rehabilitation therapy can use this to teach people what it feels like to sit or stand up straight, using vertical structures in the environment as reference points. They will use a doorpost, for example, to see what upright means and they need to teach their vestibular system this new sense of being upright (Karnath and Broetz, 2003).

Balance in school

There are careful students, there are skilful movers and there are reckless acrobats. How a student moves, on the stairs, in the playground and during PE, is partially due to how well their vestibular system processes input.

The underresponsive student

The student whose vestibular system is underresponsive can be clumsy and have a slouching posture. Control over their postural muscles is insufficient. Movements are stiff and awkward, causing this student to be more likely to bump into people and things. The latter can also happen on purpose, because bumping into things provides the student with more information. There is a big overlap in behaviour with the movement sense (proprioception). Balance and movement work together a lot.

To receive more information in the vestibular system, the student might make extra movements like swaying their head, jumping, bumping into things, rocking their chair and hanging their head upside down. When the playground has a swing set, they will spend a lot of time there, whenever they can. This student does not always pay attention to safety; their body does not sufficiently notice when it becomes unbalanced and does not transmit these alarm signals, or not in time.

The overresponsive student

The student who is overresponsive will feel dizzy faster and is more likely to feel unbalanced. This might cause them to be uncomfortable walking down stairs or playing tag, because the latter involves them running and promptly changing direction. Their body alerts them early on: you are losing your balance! They ignore the swings and the monkey bars, and they won't be getting on the slide soon either. They don't like heights and are most comfortable on smooth, hard surfaces, with both feet on the ground. This student is often late at learning to ride a bike.

SMELL

The receptors for registering scents are located in the nasal cavity. When you inhale, scents from outside the body pass these receptors. When you exhale, scents from the food and drink you've consumed pass the receptors. Because of this, the nose is an important part of tasting. You can easily test this by tasting food and drink while pinching your nose. You will not taste what you are eating or drinking as well. When you have a stuffy nose, scents can't reach the receptors.

Sense of smell plays an important part in survival; it functions as an alarm system. Your nose can detect when something is safe or unsafe. Just think of smoke, spoiled food or gas. Another important function of your sense of smell is bonding. Parent and child (unconsciously) recognize each other by their scent.

How does smell direct our life?

There are scents that are considered pleasant by most people, such as the scent of freshly baked bread and that of vanilla. By using scents in the form of perfume or by putting fresh flowers, scented candles or reed diffusers in your house you can influence your own mood, or that of others. Or perhaps you prefer not to use any scents at all, because you quickly experience them as unpleasant. Past experience with a scent plays a big part in this.

It is also important whether you've smelled this scent before, during a pleasant experience or an unpleasant or painful experience.

Additionally, you can get used to scents. The plumber is no longer bothered by the odour of the sewer they have to work in. People who don't wash themselves as often don't smell the unpleasant odours this causes.

SMELL AND SCIENCE

Businesses use scents to influence people. There are even companies that specialize in scent marketing. To do this well, it's important that they keep their target audience in mind, because there can be big differences in how people from different cultures judge scents. For example, in the United States, methyl salicylate (wintergreen) is considered a pleasant fragrance, because it was used only for mint sweets (Cain and Johnson, 1978). This same scent has a negative association in the United Kingdom, because wintergreen is used in medication (Moncrieff, 1966).

Scent influences our choice of romantic partners. Wedekind and colleagues (1995) let women smell T-shirts that were worn by men for two nights and asked them to rate the scents. The women showed a preference for the scent of those men that had different genes for coding proteins that are essential to the adaptive immune system. This shows that it might be 'just chemistry' when choosing a mate. Having different gene sets increases the survival rate of their offspring and having combinations of genes allows for a better ability to adapt to changing environments than having the same set of genes.

Smell in school

During the year, scents in a classroom may vary, partly due to the ventilation system in a school building. During the summer, windows will be open more often, resulting in more ventilation. With bad ventilation, higher temperatures will lead to more nuisance from sweaty odours. During exciting events, like the end-of-year test, some children might suffer from 'cold sweats'. In winter, moist jackets, hats, scarves and gloves will be hanging from the coat racks, while there will be relatively less ventilation. That stinks!

The underresponsive student

The student who is less aware of scents might frequently smell objects or people to receive more information. This student might like to put on (way too much) strong-smelling deodorant. For some, scented lip gloss and pens might be among their favourite things.

The overresponsive student

The student who is sensitive to scents might complain about a scent and even feel sick because of it, while others don't smell anything. Odours in the gym's changing room can cause this student to not want to follow PE at all, or they will be sure to get changed *really* fast.

TASTE

Taste receptors can be found on your tongue and in the back of your mouth, in the form of taste buds. They allow us to recognize five primary flavours: bitter, sweet, sour, salty and umami (savoury). The widespread assumption that different flavours are identified on different spots of the tongue is in-

correct. Every taste bud contains all taste receptors. Taste receptors are also found in the cheek, the roof of the mouth and the windpipe, and in organs in the body. It is still unclear what function those taste receptors have.

After food has ended up on the taste buds, information from the chemical composition is converted into an electric signal. This signal is transmitted to the brain.

To experience taste, three other senses are of importance: sense of touch to be aware of how the food feels, sense of smell to experience scents and sight to recognize the food. The four senses work together.

How does taste direct our life?

Taste largely determines the joy you experience in eating. Enjoying a tasty meal together is an important social event. Older people have fewer taste buds and don't taste their food as well, or they may experience it as bitter. This reduces their appetite. People who don't have a good sense of taste might even be living less healthily, because they add large quantities of sugar and salt to their food.

There are people who prefer varied and strong flavours. Mustard and hot sauce are often seen in their fridge. Others might enjoy less intense flavours or structures. This all depends on their sensory processing.

Taste (in combination with smell) gives a warning when food is spoiled.

TASTE AND SCIENCE

Researchers have found good reasons why children have a preference for sweet-tasting foods:

Most children have a natural preference for sweet flavours. Babies innately prefer sweet. This is for two reasons. First, in nature, bitter and sour often represent things that aren't good, like toxins. Therefore, the preference for sweet is a kind of innate survival mechanism: you'd better stay away from bitter and sour things, because they are unhealthy. However, the preference for sweet also arises from a strong need for carbohydrates (starches and sugars) to support the immense growth children go through during their first year. (De Vos, 2010)

The Japanese chemist Ikeda discovered that glutamic acid, the monosodium salt of the amino acid glutamic acid, is the substance that's responsible for umami flavour (savoury). His discovery was immediately put into practice. Using monosodium glutamate (or MSG) as a flavour enhancer has since become common practice in Asian cuisine. In the early 20th century, MSG was extracted from seaweed. Nowadays, MSG is produced by fermenting molasses from sugar cane, sugar beets, starches or corn (Kurihara, 2009).

Taste in school

Taste is less likely to be an issue in class. Students usually bring fruit, food and drinks to school that parents know they will like.

The underresponsive student

This student doesn't taste their food as well, which can reduce their appetite. They also prefer foods with strong flavours in their lunch box, like crisps or a chocolate bar. They'd rather not have a slice of white bread and bland cheese.

The overresponsive student

The student who is pickier about their food will perhaps refuse snacks that are being handed out, because they don't like them. However, because treats handed out in class are often sweet, they probably won't refuse them that often. Sweet is a flavour that even overresponsive people generally enjoy.

INTEROCEPTION

The term 'interoception' means 'experiencing the inside'. It describes the sense that registers what we sense in organs and other tissues in our body, for instance (the lining of) the stomach, bladder, heart or intestines. The sensors are located throughout your body. Some locations have a lot, for instance the lining of organs such as the bladder. A large proportion of the interoceptive signals are processed fully automatically by the nervous system. Reactions to these sensations are a balance between actions of which you are aware and unaware. You can be aware of being tired and then go to sleep. You can be unaware of a potential danger: your pupils have already widened, even before you are aware of being fearful. Interoceptive signals usually are treated as having priority over signals from other senses, because they are linked to survival (food, excreting, danger, reproduction). Understanding signals from interoception are important for self-regulating behaviour to help you feel better (if you feel 'full', stopping eating will make you feel better).

How does interoception direct our life?

To be able to function in daily life, you need to be able to interpret interoceptive signals that require action. For instance, you need to be able to match the feeling of a tense bladder to the experience of emptying your bladder and to go to the toilet in a timely manner. To not become dehydrated, you need to learn what being thirsty feels like, so you can get a glass of water. Do you have shaky legs and 'butterflies' in your stomach? You may be nervous, ill or in love. Emotions can arise from interoceptive stimuli. A child with an asthma attack, for example, can panic because they have to gasp for breath. In a weakened form, a child with a cold may feel nervous because of this. By learning to match what you feel inside your body to a situation or emotion, you can take the required action to survive, for instance run away because you experience fear.

INTEROCEPTION AND SCIENCE

In their research, Umeda and colleagues (2016) link higher interoceptive accuracy (being able to better sense the physiological condition of your body) with an ability to better invoke prospective memories (PM). A PM is a memory that is retained to be used for future intentions. Participants with better interoceptive accuracy showed better PM task performance. These results show that this higher cognition task (PM recall) is dependent on the sense of interoception (Umeda *et al.*, 2016).

Contemporary experiments demonstrate the neural and mental representation of internal bodily sensations as integral for the experience of emotions; those individuals with heightened interoception tend to experience emotions with greater intensity (Barrett *et al.*, 2004).

Interoceptive signals can guide and inform without fully penetrating conscious awareness. 'In addition, interoceptive dysregulation appears to underlie alexithymia – difficulty identifying one's own emotions and sensations (Brewer *et al.*, 2016). Alexithymia is a common hallmark of psychological disorders such as Autism Spectrum Conditions that present with social difficulties (Bird and Cook, 2013)' (Arnold, Winkielman and Dobkins, 2019).

 # Interoception in school

When students get hungry, need to go to the toilet or are in love, they will be less able to pay attention to the teacher and to their work. Signals from interoception are interpreted as being the number one priority by the brain, because they are important for survival. Therefore interoceptive signals get most or all attention.

The underresponsive student

This student will get restless when they need to eat or drink, but they are unable to translate the signal to needing food or being thirsty. They will have a harder time with toilet-training and may have accidents past an age where this usually has stopped occurring. This student may not feel scrapes and bruises. They may 'all of a sudden' become furious, because they did not feel the irritation and anger build up. This feeling has been building in their body, but they are not aware of it until it has passed the 'bursting' point. Or a student will deny being angry, whilst having tightly closed fists, tension in their body and 'thunder' in their face, just because they do not perceive these anger signals.

The overresponsive student

This student experiences signals from their body as very strong. A slightly filled bladder will feel like it's about to burst, so the student will often need to use the toilet. They will respond more strongly than seems necessary, for instance when they are lightly bumped against. This student may be very irritated when feeling mild hunger or thirst.

The predictive brain

There are many factors involved in experiencing sensations, for instance past experience, the sensory input filter we speak about in this book, and safety and danger mechanisms in the brain. One of the factors is 'the predictive brain', where the brain predicts what you should experience, based on past experience with sensory input.

It would take too much time and energy to only respond to the sensory input of the moment, therefore the brain makes predictions based on the many experiences you have had with sensory input. What you experience (as being true) is based on these predictions, instead of on what is actually there (the factual truth). The predictions are not always correct, but the brain usually corrects based on the incoming sensory input. This way the predictions are 'weighed against' the actual input. But the brain may also decide not to correct based on the actual input. The brain will then filter in a way that only the sensory input that matches the prediction is processed and experienced, making the prediction 'true' (Feldman Barret, 2017).

PART II

GETTING STARTED: WHAT CAN YOU DO?

If all went well, you are now more than ready and cannot wait to support your students. That is why this book was written: to help you respond to behaviour in school which has to do with under- and overresponsivity. You will be the one to work on this, but of course we will guide you, so you have the greatest chance of success.

In this part we use frames so you can look things up quickly. You can pick up the book in the classroom and quickly find the information you need at that moment: practical tips, an activating or calming strategy, in the classroom or outside the classroom. We provide many different strategies so you can choose what best suits you, the student and the situation. If you want to know more about a certain strategy or about tools, you can find information at the end of this part.

4

Before You Begin

What's this chapter about?

This chapter is a manual to help you utilize the strategies described in Chapters 5–10 appropriately. To get started, we have created a convenient SPI-viewing guide, which helps you choose a fitting strategy: activating or calming. We also revisit the 'Fan-model' introduced in Chapter 1, which helps the student become aware of their personal input needs. By means of two outlines, we explain how you can tell if an inactive or hyperactive student is under- or overresponsive. Furthermore, we explain what applying the strategies can look like in daily life, and we answer practical questions you may have before getting started.

The SPI-viewing guide

The SPI-viewing guide helps you determine which strategy is required. You use the viewing guide when you notice disruptive behaviour, or behaviour that shows your student isn't functioning optimally in the current situation. First, the SPI-Glasses will help you classify the behaviour and then you can check if a strategy is needed. In Chapter 2, we discussed which behaviours suggest being under- and overresponsive. The SPI-viewing guide along with a list of these behaviours is available to download.

The SPI-viewing guide

The child is displaying disruptive behaviour

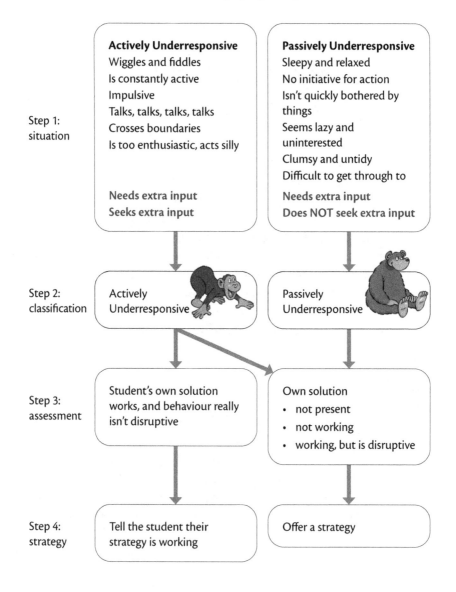

Step 1: situation

Actively Underresponsive	**Passively Underresponsive**
Wiggles and fiddles	Sleepy and relaxed
Is constantly active	No initiative for action
Impulsive	Isn't quickly bothered by things
Talks, talks, talks, talks	Seems lazy and uninterested
Crosses boundaries	Clumsy and untidy
Is too enthusiastic, acts silly	Difficult to get through to
Needs extra input	**Needs extra input**
Seeks extra input	**Does NOT seek extra input**

Step 2: classification

Actively Underresponsive

Passively Underresponsive

Step 3: assessment

Student's own solution works, and behaviour really isn't disruptive

Own solution
- not present
- not working
- working, but is disruptive

Step 4: strategy

Tell the student their strategy is working

Offer a strategy

98

The child is displaying disruptive behaviour

Step 1: situation

Actively Overresponsive
Not flexible, wants routine
Makes decisions easily
Notices every (little) change
Is easily annoyed
Refuses, often doesn't want to come (or play) along
Wants to determine how things go

Is bothered by input
Avoids input

Passively Overresponsive
Responds to everything in their environment
Easily angered, grumbles, cries
Impressions last for a long time
Likes to be on their own
Things often 'suddenly' become too much
Becomes fearful easily

Is bothered by input
Does NOT avoid input

Step 2: classification

Actively Overresponsive

Passively Overresponsive

Step 3: assessment

Student's own solution works, and behaviour really isn't disruptive

Own solution
• not present
• not working
• works, but is disruptive

Step 4: strategy

Tell the student their strategy is working

Offer a strategy

With the following example, we will show you how the SPI-viewing guide works.

1. The student is balancing their chair on two legs during reading time. You're thinking: Sit still please! In short, you notice disruptive behaviour, *Step 1* in the diagram.
2. This is when you put on your SPI-Glasses and consider if the behaviour can be linked to under- or overresponsivity. Is the student behaving like this to stay focused, to regulate their alertness? Is the student active to receive more input? Probably. An underresponsive student can apply rocking their chair for extra input. This is *Step 2* in the diagram, classification.
3. Then, *Step 3*, assessing the behaviour: is the behaviour truly disruptive? The student is moving around a bit, isn't touching anyone and is quiet. No, it's not that disruptive after all.
4. Now, you arrive at *Step 4*, choosing a strategy: telling the student their strategy is working.

However, sometimes the student's behaviour *is* disruptive. It's nice that the student is trying to regulate their alertness, but if the chair legs squeak with every movement this is very disruptive. Similarly, if the student moves a lot, or talks, talks, talks, talks, talks... Through the SPI-viewing guide, you will now end up at a different strategy. This helps you offer the student – and thus yourself and other students as well! – a good, non-disruptive alternative.

> **You put on your SPI-Glasses and see something is wrong with sensory processing.**

Another example: the student is slouching in their chair; they are quiet and withdrawn. Typical underresponsive behaviour, which the student isn't trying to change themselves. You once again put on your SPI-Glasses and see something is wrong with sensory processing. By going through the SPI-viewing guide, you know you can offer an activating strategy.

You can test at which classification of the student you end up and if this is the right classification. Chapter 11 offers opportunities to practise classifying disruptive behaviour with the SPI-viewing guide. We provide examples of student behaviour in different situations. If you want to practise right now, you can skip ahead to Chapter 11.

The Fan-model: Extra help with Step 2, classification

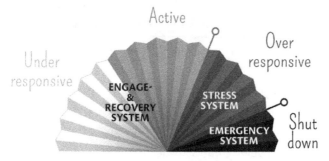

Fan-model by Thoonsen and van der Gaag (2021)

Through the Fan-model, the student will learn to recognize the state their sensory processing is in. Without a visual aid, this can be complicated. It can be difficult for a child to indicate when they are overresponsive, for example. Consequently, they may 'suddenly' become overwhelmed. When that happens, your student has missed certain signals. Therefore, it's nice if they themselves can indicate if they are under- or overresponsive, or when they notice they have reached a limit. You, the teacher, will also learn to recognize the signals better and sooner, which means you can warn the student in time and you can prevent them from becoming overwhelmed.

When you think your student isn't fully aware of when they experience too much or too little input, go ahead and use the Fan-model to practise together. The fan shows you how they are doing, which system is active and therefore if they are maybe under- or overresponsive. Can they do their task, or is that not quite possible? If they can't, is this because they lack input, are they functioning in the left-hand part of the fan, or are they experiencing too much input and are they functioning in the right-hand or far-right part?

The student now has a helpful tool to check for themselves if they need something to (continue to) feel comfortable, so they can do what they need to in that moment. You can respond to what the student needs: more or less input.

TO DO: THE FAN-MODEL

Having read and discussed this tutorial, you can start using the Fan-model. Do this in specific situations, for example during independent working time, arts and crafts or when doing group activities.

Further explanation on the use of the Fan-model can be found at www.DutchSensorySolutions.com.

It depends on the situation

The Fan-model parts differ in each situation with regards to energy and behaviour. When giving a presentation, it's okay to be a bit nervous and function in the right-hand zone. This makes you more active and enables you to respond well to your classmates' questions. In that moment, this could mean you are a bit over-active. Therefore, a very active student will indicate the right-hand part of the fan is unfolded a bit. However, when they are *so* active that they no longer respond to classmates who want to ask them a question, the right-hand part is unfolded too much and the student may even unfold the very far right corner.

When a student is enjoying the sunshine in the playground, it's okay if they are very relaxed, because that is exactly right for the situation. Consequently, a student who is relaxing in the sun will show that the left-hand side is unfolded a bit. But if they don't notice break is over and everybody is supposed to go back to their classroom, that side is unfolded too much.

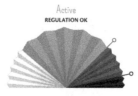

After having practised using the Fan-model several times, your student will most likely be able to indicate themselves what state they are in. And perhaps, after a while, without even using the fan. They will then also be capable of applying some strategies independently, so they can start self-regulating.

The SPI-viewing guide: Extra help with Step 2, classification

When dealing with a hyperactive or very passive student (who is absorbed in their own world) it can be difficult to recognize if they are under- or overresponsive. Below, we explain how you can tell the difference by looking at physical characteristics.

The hyperactive student

When we say 'hyperactive', we mean a student who is *so* active that they cannot focus on the task at hand. They started out by seeking more input but overshot the mark. They may constantly be standing up and walking around, no longer paying attention to their task. Perhaps pencils or books fall on the floor, but they don't notice.

This student has lost track of the input surrounding them; it engulfs them. This makes them feel bad, but it's difficult for them to get out of this situation on their own.

The hyperactive student may at first come across as an underresponsive student who is actively looking for more input. But the overresponsive student can be hyperactive too, because they are experiencing a lot of stress. Often, it's possible to tell the difference, because an underresponsive and hyperactive student is moving a lot, 'stomping around'. An overresponsive and hyperactive student predominantly moves in a nervous manner. They are clumsy and active, but their movements aren't as big as those of the underresponsive student.

Because it can be tricky to determine whether a hyperactive student is under- or overresponsive, we will discuss four characteristics below, which will help you tell the difference. These four points – which can also be found in the following diagram – describe what the eyes, breathing and muscular tension look like and which emotions you can expect. The last row of the diagram shows what you can do.

	Hyperactive and underresponsive	Hyperactive and overresponsive
Eyes	Wide open and enthusiastic (seeking input)	Wide open, stressed/fearful (picking up all signals)
Breathing	Relaxed abdominal breathing	Tense chest breathing
Muscle tension	Relaxed muscles, enthusiastic, fluid movements	Tense muscles, shoulders hunched, chaotic movements
Emotions	Hyper and enthusiastic The student is 'losing it', cannot stop themselves Extreme emotions, such as super happy	Hyper and stressed 'Has a meltdown' Grumbling/complaining, angry or crying Not flexible The student is in survival mode
Supportive action	First, help them to calm down Then, offer less intensely activating input (that is not disruptive for the student and their environment)	Decrease input Offer calming input Remove from situation

The underresponsive and hyperactive student mostly shows extreme enthusiasm and boisterous behaviour. This student is having fun. However, they are a little *too* enthusiastic, which negatively affects them and the environment. The student 'loses it' and shows extreme emotions.

The overresponsive and hyperactive student mostly shows stress and extreme nervousness. This student is overwhelmed by all the sensory input and is feeling uncomfortable. They are in survival mode.

The student living in their own little world
By this, we mean a student who does nothing when a situation requires active engagement. This student fails to take action. They don't respond to their environment, including your encouragement to do something.

You would think this student is underresponsive. There simply isn't enough input coming in to get and keep them awake. But an overresponsive student can *also* be in their own little world. The student has become so overresponsive that they retreat completely, to ensure no more input can get in. In this case, you check the eyes, breathing, muscle tension and emotion as well, to see if you are dealing with an under- or overresponsive student.

	In their own world and underresponsive	In their own world and overresponsive
Eyes	Sleepy/sluggish (little to no input is getting in)	Avoids direct eye contact
Breathing	Relaxed abdominal breathing	Tense chest breathing
Muscle tension	Relaxed muscles, slouched posture, sluggish movements	Tense muscles, shoulders hunched, when they move, the movements are jerky. Body and head turned away from the hustle and bustle
Emotions	Not showing	Fearful (can have bursts of extreme emotions)
Supportive action	Offer activating input (that is not disruptive for the student and their environment)	Decrease input. Offer calming input. Remove from situation

The underresponsive student who is off in their own little world mostly shows sleepy/sluggish behaviour and is relaxed. It can be difficult to connect with this student; you have to call them multiple times before they hear that the task is at an end and their stuff needs to be put away.

The overresponsive student who is off in their own little world will show stress and tension. This student is overwhelmed by all the sensory input and feels threatened. They will retreat and become unresponsive.

The SPI-viewing guide: Extra help with Step 3, the assessment
What do you do? Let it go or choose a strategy?
When you have established whether the student is under- or overresponsive, Step 3 will help you decide if you should interfere. You have three choices:

- Don't offer a strategy, because the student's behaviour is helping them gain better input balance and is not disruptive. They have come up with their own solution and it's working.
- Choose a strategy for an underresponsive student, because they will need more input to be comfortable and be able to participate.

- Choose a strategy for an overresponsive student, because the amount of input around them is bothering them and they need to be calmed down and/or be exposed to less input.

If it ends with Step 3

If the student has their own strategy to restore their input balance and it's working fine, you will be done after Step 3. Or so you thought...

This is a great time to tell this student: 'It's fantastic you know exactly what you need!' Because this is the desired end goal: that they recognize their needs and come up with solutions themselves. It is important to acknowledge this.

The information about the *four* types only matters, because the behaviours of an active and passive type are different. It is important that you can recognize this to be able to tell if a student is under- or overresponsive. This is what you base your strategy on. The strategy itself doesn't depend on active or passive behaviour. Eventually, you will find just two categories with our strategies:

- strategies for the underresponsive student
- strategies for the overresponsive student.

The SPI-viewing guide: Extra help with Step 4, the strategy
How to get off to a good start?

Well begun is half done. With help from the instructions on the next page, you will be off to a good start. By preparing your students and coming to clear agreements, you will ensure the use of strategies will not cause commotion.

First of all, you tell the students why you will be working with short activities that affect how they feel. We advise you to spend one or two lessons on sensory processing, so the students will understand why these new things are happening in their class. A short way to explain the goal of these strategies is by telling them there are moments where their body is too sleepy to learn properly, and there are other moments where they are too restless or stressed to learn properly. A student who is too sleepy to do what they have to do needs to be activated, and a student who is too restless or stressed will need to be calmed down, or maybe even 'let off steam' to release tension. The goal is to get the student to be calm and focused enough to perform their task as needed. The goal is always to get the student's alertness level to suit their task.

Then you provide a few examples of strategies and try to mention things the student is already doing of their own accord, such as fiddling with a rubber band while they are reading.

Afterwards, you discuss what the results of a strategy can be. 'When you are fiddling with a rubber band while reading, you are able to stay focused.' You will tell them that it may not work the first time. 'Let's try this a couple of times, shall we? Because we can't really tell if it helps or not without practising and trying it a few times.'

> **The goal is always to get the student's alertness level to suit their task.**

Instructions for a good start

- See if the student can think of what they need when a situation arises. 'What could help you?' and 'How can we make that happen?'
- Practise with your students, so they can execute the strategies appropriately.
- When individual strategies are applied, you will explain these to all students, so they understand what that one student is doing and why. Make separate arrangements with the student who needs these strategies, enabling them to self-regulate.
- Explain how the students should behave while strategies are executed:
  - Will they execute the strategy in silence?
  - Are they allowed to touch each other?
  - What will happen to the furniture?
- Come to clear agreements with the students. Decide whether they are allowed to fiddle with a shoelace or rubber band while you are reading to the class, and if they are allowed to get up to stretch during independent working moments.
- Ask the student to pay attention to if they are feeling better and are better equipped to perform their task.
- Tell them how the strategy is finalized:

- Separate arrangements have been made with the student for individual strategies.
- It's best that strategies involving the entire class always end the same way, for example: everybody is back in their chairs at the count of three, in silence. In Chapter 9, in 'Fixed rituals in class', we will reflect on this extensively.
- Steadily build up the use of strategies, so you and your students can familiarize yourselves with them. Don't try too many new things at once.
- Slowly expand on the strategies you are using. Strategies involving the entire class can first be applied during reading time only, then also during circle time, then also during art, etc. The individual strategy can first be applied to two students, then four, and so on.

Allow a trial period for each strategy. When the strategy has been practised and has been applied for a week, you should be able to see results. The student should now really be capable of focusing better on their task. If you don't see these changes, it's time to try out a different strategy.

The whole class, or individually

You choose to involve the whole class:

- when the students are noisy and this doesn't go well with the task set for them. Then you can use a calming strategy involving the entire class. For instance, when you are discussing a test and the kids are getting rowdy, you can ask all students to close their eyes and lead them in a calming breathing exercise.
- when the students are dozing off when they really should be paying attention. Then you'll use an activating strategy involving the entire class.

  When the students have had to listen or read for an extended time, they need to be activated before they can continue. You should plan moments like this at least every 15 minutes when students have to sit still for a prolonged period. Standing next to their chair for a minute and running on the spot is done quickly and has scientifically been proven to have a positive effect on the learning abilities of students (see 'Science about movement and learning' in Chapter 7).

You pick an individual strategy:

- for the student who is bothered by their problematic sensory processing *the entire day*.

  This student is suffering from problems with sensory processing at various times during the day; there is no set pattern. You probably recognize this student. They're the one who gets distracted sometimes when they should be listening to a fellow student's presentation, a clip showing on the digital whiteboard or the teacher explaining something. This same student will drift off at some other moment, while working independently.

  You can practise strategies with this student. When you notice they are becoming distracted when listening, you can, for instance, give them an agreed upon signal to write down key words from what they are being told at that moment. During independent working time they could always grab hearing protection which they will use on their own initiative or after receiving a signal from you.

- for the student who is bothered by their sensory processing *at fixed moments*.

  This student shows disruptive behaviour during specific activities or times of the day. This is the student who is *so* hyper when entering the classroom every morning that they disturb you and their classmates by talking and running around the classroom. That student who always needs a little extra encouragement during independent reading time. Do the exact same thing with this student: practise the strategies and come to agreements about their execution, and decide together at what moments and with what degree of independence the student can execute the strategies. In the morning, for example, they could take the chairs off the tables and wipe the chalkboard clean; prior to independent reading time they could run up and down the stairs twice and while reading they will fiddle with a rubber band.

How do you support the individual student?

You should come to individual agreements with the student beforehand about when and how they can execute their strategies. After practising a few times, the student has a firm understanding of what the possibilities are and they can execute the strategies independently. Should the student be unable to estimate on their own when they need to use a strategy, you and the student can think of a way for you to help them with this. For example: when the student exhibits disruptive behaviour, you will point to images – which the student can make themselves – or you will act out the strategy, for instance, by pretending you are putting on hearing protection.

The duration of a strategy

You can choose from strategies ranging from a length of a few seconds to a few minutes, although you can make most strategies last as long as you want. When reading the strategy, it will become clear how much time is needed. This will never be more than a few minutes and will regularly be less than a minute. Besides that, you are free to do as you choose. You can:

- have a student jump in place three times, or ten times
- during a breathing exercise, have a student breathe in and out three times before you continue the class, or have the students pay attention to their breathing longer and with their eyes closed.

You make a choice depending on what's needed (activating or calming) and what you have space for; not just physically, but especially in terms of time. When you have used the strategies a few times, you will have a good idea of the possibilities. And the better you have practised the strategies, the less time they will take.

Interrupting class – or not

Take a situation where you are reading a story to the entire class. Some students are starting to wiggle and fiddle. They are exhibiting restless behaviour. You assess their behaviour and the situation. You think they might be drifting off a little or they are self-regulating to be able to keep following the story, but they are doing this in a disruptive manner. These students need to be activated. You can stop reading and start stretching with the whole class, after which you continue reading. You can also choose to ask the restless students to grab their kneading putty and fiddle with that in silence.

The answer to the question 'Do I use a strategy during the lesson, or do we stop what we are doing?' depends on a couple of considerations:

- Is everyone working independently?
  Choose individual strategies. During independent working time you'll probably choose not to disrupt the work.
- Are all students ready to take a break – i.e. there are many restless students – and/or are you in-between two activities?
  This is a great time for a strategy involving the whole class.
- Is there one student who needs to be activated or calmed?
  Choose an individual strategy.

How do you choose the right strategy?

First of all, you will have decided if you need a strategy for under- or overresponsivity, if this needs to applied to the entire class or individually and where this strategy will be executed: on the chair, next to the chair or in the classroom. However, within these choices there are several different possibilities. Which strategy do you choose then?

- Perhaps you don't need to choose, because the student has already made a choice. See what type of self-regulation they are already using:
  - If their own strategy is effective, you will not have to make a choice at all. All you have to do is to give positive feedback, so you will both know what their successful strategy is.
  - If their own strategy is not working or if it is disruptive, you will offer an alternative option.
- Look at your own sensory processing when choosing a strategy. If you don't like having a lot of movement or fuss around you, choose 'in your seat' strategies.
- Look at practical issues: no drinking water when using the computer, for example.
- Talk to the student: what do they think they will need to be able to continue with their task? You can give them a choice, if the

student has not yet had much practice with using strategies. Limit the choice to two options; making a decision can also be a taxing job.

- Start with the strategies that appeal to you most, and that fit in the room when it comes to space and materials. For instance, you could choose an activating strategy involving the entire class, where the students march on the spot. This strategy is appealing to you and there is enough space in the classroom to execute it.

- See if the strategy has the desired effect. Maybe the students aren't responding the way you want them to. They might be getting more active, but the marching is making them rather hyperactive.

   If this is still the case after having practised a couple of times, choose a different strategy. For example, this time you will start stretching and try to touch the ceiling. Very activating, but everyone remains nice and quiet.

- Decide what's best in that moment:
   - Do you want a sitting-down or standing-up strategy?
   - Is there time and space to move around the classroom?
   - How long can the strategy last?
   - What would you yourself prefer to be doing?

There are so many strategies that there is bound to be one for every moment and situation. And after having read all our examples, you might think of even more strategies that suit you and your students perfectly.

> *When you are in doubt about whether your student is under- or overresponsive, always choose a strategy for an overresponsive student.*

What if you are in doubt about the student being under- or overresponsive?

A strategy is necessary, because the student isn't feeling comfortable and can't handle their task. But you are in doubt about whether they are under- or overresponsive. Therefore, you don't know what type of strategy to choose. In this case, you will *always* choose a strategy for an overresponsive student. It is never a bad thing to remove input, but it can be counterproductive to add input at the wrong time. The reasons for this are outlined below.

Strategies for overresponsive students are generally calming

- The effect of a calming strategy on an underresponsive student: they are even less alert, because input is removed when they need it. Not ideal, but not damaging. When this happens, at least you don't have to doubt the situation anymore. You can now see more clearly that the student is underresponsive and you will consequently choose a fitting strategy. Compare it to: you are lying on the couch, feeling groggy, and you get a cup of tea. It doesn't change the grogginess; it might even make you feel groggier, but it's not a problem either.
- The effect of a calming strategy on an overresponsive student: they will start to feel better. This is good.

Strategies for underresponsive students are generally activating

- The effect of an activating strategy on an underresponsive student: it enables them to better respond to their environment. Fine.
- But...the effect of an activating strategy on an overresponsive student is even more stress and tension. This is very unpleasant for the student and you want to prevent this. Compare it to: you are lying on the couch with a headache and someone puts on really loud music. This will make you feel worse.

As you can see, offering an activating strategy to an overresponsive student can exacerbate the situation. The student, who is already overresponsive, is receiving more sensory input and cannot process this. You want to prevent this, so, when in doubt, first choose a strategy suited to the overresponsive student.

Pay close attention to the first response of the student to the strategy you are offering, and if necessary, adjust the strategy accordingly.

What do you need?

In theory, you only need yourself and the students. Most of the strategies are very easy to understand and execute. You don't have to download video clips, mark the floor with x's or move to specific songs in special ways. The only things you have to do are:

- notice disruptive behaviour
- put on SPI-Glasses
- choose a strategy
- witness success.

There are strategies that use special tools, such as a balance cushion or chewing materials. The rest use general basic household supplies where possible. The student can fiddle with shoelaces, feel Velcro strips and wiggle their legs while sitting in their chair.

At what pace should a strategy be executed?

A couple of the strategies from the next chapters can be found under both activating and calming strategies. This has to do with the fact that the way a strategy is executed influences whether it has an activating or calming effect. There are a few rules for this:

Activating	Calming
Move quickly	Move slowly
Vary	Repeat
Move irregularly	Move rhythmically
Changes	Not too much variation
Unexpected things	Expected things
New things	Familiar things
Brief activity	Longer lasting activity

In the following cartoons, you will see that the same strategy can be executed in an activating and calming way.

BREATHING EXERCISE, ACTIVATING

Don't tell the students in advance how many times the exercise will be repeated. Repeat two to five times.

BREATHING EXERCISE, CALMING

PRESSING THE PALMS OF YOUR HANDS TOGETHER, ACTIVATING

PRESSING THE PALMS OF YOUR HANDS TOGETHER, CALMING

Tools

Strategies for which tools can be used will be regularly discussed in the next chapters. Many of these tools are available in regular stores.

What's the difference between energizers and relaxation exercises?

The internet offers an abundance of energizers and relaxation exercises to use in class. These games and exercises can be played on the digital whiteboard and/or contain directions for the teacher. By doing the exercises and playing the games, the students will regain energy or will be able to relax. You may have a few favourite energizers and relaxation exercises of your own which you use in class. The goals of the energizers and relaxation exercises partly overlap with the goals of our strategies. However, there are differences between them.

Strategies	Energizers and relaxation exercises
Are prompted by disruptive behaviour The cause of this behaviour is under- or overresponsivity	Aren't always meant as a solution to certain behaviour
Are deployed for a specific purpose	Don't have to be part of a specific vision
Are executed with the whole class or individually	Are generally done with the whole class
Can be executed independently	Are performed under supervision
Can be executed while doing class work	Are mainly done between activities
Often take less than one minute	Generally need more (preparation) time

It needs getting used to

And then, suddenly, there's a student getting up during class to stretch, while another does push-ups in-between maths exercises and a third is wearing a necklace they are chewing on.

When you start using strategies to support sensory processing, the classroom is going to look a little different. Usually, hats, hoodies and sunglasses are not accepted in class. But when viewed through SPI-Glasses, they are incredibly useful tools for the student who is easily distracted and can't get to work because of this. Because you are now able to look at behaviour through SPI-Glasses, you can see the advantages of this strategy. You no longer see a hoody, but a protection device against input, a tool to help combat interfering input. It would be a waste not to use such a good tool. Based on this idea, you can come to agreements with the students about when and how long they can use such tools.

To prevent confusion ('Miss Lynn allows kids to wear their hoody, so weird'), it's a good idea to announce this new approach. Then, everybody will know why hats, hoodies or sunglasses can be worn in certain situations, for example during independent working time.

5

Strategies in the Classroom

What's this chapter about?

In this chapter, we provide more than two hundred strategies for you to execute in class to improve sensory processing. We categorize the strategies as activating and calming. In addition, we categorize the strategies according to where they can be done in the classroom – sitting on or standing next to your chair or moving around the classroom.

 ## TO DO: ACTIVATE

While reading this book, your attention could be dropping a little as well. You are actually underresponsive. A good time to test the waters and try out one of our strategies! Take some time after each strategy to experience how it affects your alertness and how long this effect lasts.

- Put the palms of your hands together, fingers pointing upwards, and push them against each other as hard as you can, while continuing to breathe calmly (hold for ten seconds and repeat the exercise three times).
- Only do this second one if you don't have back or neck problems: stand up from your chair and drop yourself back into the chair.
- Take three powerful breaths. Breathe in through your nose and out through your mouth. When breathing out for the last time, make it extra powerful.
- Stand next to your chair and run on the spot for ten seconds.

These are short and simple activities which will provide long-lasting energy. They give a taste of the possibilities and how fast they work.

Activating and calming

One student may need extra input, whereas another may need input removed. Therefore, we have categorized the strategies as activating and calming. Activating is to be used for the underresponsive student, calming for the overresponsive student.

- Some of the calming strategies are meant for blowing off steam, for example by moving or fiddling with something. Assessing what the student needs can be done with the help of the SPI viewing guide in Chapter 4.
- Some strategies can be executed in both an activating and a calming manner. Revisit the section in Chapter 4, 'At what pace should a strategy be executed?' This explains how certain strategies can have both an activating and calming effect.
- A few strategies will be further explained in Chapter 7. There, we will explain why some strategies are activating or calming, tell you more about helpful tools and provide information from scientific studies concerning some of the strategies.

Notes

- When 'you' is used in the strategies, it refers to the student. You, the teacher, provide instruction and demonstrate the exercise.
- In the exercises, you will see some words are *italicized*. This indicates mention of tools that aren't general household items and should therefore be organized before starting.
- The locations where the strategies should be executed have been divided into different categories: in your chair, next to your chair or in the classroom.
- * Our favourite strategies have been marked with an asterisk.

In your chair

First, we will look at the strategies that can be executed by the student while sitting in their chair. They are predominantly very simple and short activities. Most of these strategies can be executed while the student is thinking, listening or reading. They are highly suited to individual execution. Nevertheless, most strategies can also be executed with the entire class.

The *underresponsive* student needs a little extra input every now and then. This extra input stimulates them to get or stay focused on their work. Activating input doesn't always require them to leave their chair. Below, you will find different options for the student to fulfil their extra input requirements while staying seated.

Activating in your chair

Fingers

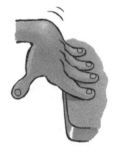

- Overstretch your fingers (by pushing against them or pressing them down on the table or in your lap).
- Squeeze your hands, twist and fiddle with your fingers, press your thumb into the palm of your other hand.
- * Fiddle with silent materials, such as a *kneaded eraser, rubber bands* or a *shoelace.*
- Create a figure or necklace from *paperclips*, then untangle the paperclips.
- Fiddle with the soft side (the soft side doesn't make much noise) of *Velcro* which has been attached to the underside of your desk.
- Craft something, using *finger paint, glue, adhesive tape* and other sticky materials.
- Rapidly squeeze a *kneaded eraser*, or a *rubber (stress) ball.*
- Move a pen or pencil through the fingers of one hand.
- Play 'Simon Says', with finger movements.
- Tap your fingers on the table, repeating the rhythm the teacher or a fellow student is tapping (the overresponsive student might want to put on hearing protection during this exercise).

Head

- Grab your hair and softly pull it.
- Rub your face firmly with your fingers or your entire hand.
- Softly pull your ears; grab your ears between your thumb and forefinger and firmly massage them.
- Firmly and quickly rub your fingers on your forehead and your temples.
- Firmly and in a controlled manner, shake your head 'no' (we use 'no',

because firmly shaking 'yes' can be painful when the head is overextended backwards).

* Move your head: bend your head forwards, backwards and to the sides, turn your head clockwise and anticlockwise.

Mouth

* Chew on specially designed *chewing tools.*
• Chew (pieces of) *sugar free chewing gum.*
• Drink water from a *water bottle*:
  – drink water with *lemon or lime*
  – drink *ice water*
  – drink through a *straw.*
• Bring activating items in your lunch/snack box:
  – crunchy foods, such as carrots and apples
  – heavy-duty chewing foods, such as raisins, dried fruits, sugar free chewing gum
  – citrus fruits and drinks
  – strong flavours (mustard, hot sauce, wasabi)
  – yoghurt or apple sauce, to drink through a straw.
• Take a couple of deep breaths. Breathe in through your nose, hold for two seconds and breathe out through your mouth. Repeat this two to five times. Breathe out strongly the last time.
• Use a *straw* to blow *cotton balls* over the table (into an open goal).
• Put a pencil on the table and blow this across on the table, taking care it stays on the table.

Arms

- Wave.
- * Put the palms of your hands together, fingers pointing upwards, and push them together as hard as you can, while keeping on breathing.
- Push your hands firmly and quickly against your body (on your legs, on your arms, against each other).
- * Push yourself up slowly (put your hands on the seat of your chair, lift your feet off the ground and push, so your bottom doesn't touch the seat).
- Try to lift your chair by its seat, while sitting on it.
- Stretch your body completely.

Legs

- Push your feet against an *elastic band* tied between the feet of the chair or the table.
- Sit with your legs crossed.
- Lift your heels and toes a few times, as high as you can, alternating feet.
- Roll your feet (wearing socks or barefoot) over a spiky *massage ball*.
- Put one foot/lower leg on the seat of your chair and sit on it.
- Wrap your legs around the legs of the chair or table and tense your leg muscles.
- Put one leg over the other and wiggle the upper leg.

Posture

- Change your sitting position: for example, slouch down with your legs spread wide, put your legs over each other or put one leg up.
- Turn your chair around, sit down, straddling the chair, with your belly against the back of the chair.
- Do the 'back-of-the-chair stretch'. See 'This is how you do it', below.
* Sit on a *balance cushion* for a short while (maximum of half an hour at a time).
- Balance on two legs of your chair.
- Lie down across your chair, on your back, with your head leaning down.

Other

- Listen to *music* on an *MP3 player* or other *music carrier*.
- Write down key words about what is being taught that moment.
- Use, if possible, an appealing notebook and book, and a pretty pen with lots of colours.
- Use a *pen with bumps or ridges on the outside*.
- Use a *coloured and/or scented pen*.

This is how you do it

Turn to one side, grab the back of the chair with both your hands and try to turn your upper body as far as you can while your knees keep pointing forward.

The *overresponsive* student needs time every now and then to recover from all the input. A calming strategy ensures they will calm down and allow them to learn. The student can perform most of these strategies alone and independently, without any fuss, while sitting in their own chair.

Calming down in your chair
Fingers

- Use *hand lotion* with a pleasant scent. Smell your hand regularly. Do this during a difficult task or to mask unpleasant smells.
- Slowly squeeze a *rubber (stress) ball*.
* Fiddle with quiet materials, such as *kneaded erasers*, a *rubber band*, *koosh ball* or *shoelace*.
- Play string games: make figures using a *piece of wool or string*.
- Craft something in a way that you don't get sticky stuff on your fingers:
    - make sure you are the one cutting and tearing during the crafts projects, instead of being the one gluing things
    - use a *brush* instead of your fingers during finger painting
    - use *paint markers* instead of paint
    - use a *tape dispenser* instead of loose tape
    - use *tweezers* instead of your fingers to hold things.
- Take a *big ring* from a key chain and put it around your fingers, one by one.
- Tap each finger against your thumb three times, both hands separately or at the same time.
- Use the *sign alphabet* to spell out your name.
- Spread your fingers as far as you can, make fists and relax. Repeat a couple of times.
* Entwine your fingers, separate them, play with them.
- Squeeze one hand with your other hand, squeeze your fingers and then do this with your other hand.

Head

- Very slowly pull your ears; down, to the side and up. Close your eyes and make sure your breathing is calm.
- Calmly rub your temples and your fore-head with your fingertips.
- Softly massage your head with your fingers: put your fingers on your head and slowly circle them around. You can close your eyes while doing this.
- Rub your face calmly with the flats of your hands, out from your nose to your ears.
- Put your hands on top of your head and press down softly.
- Pull up the *hood* of your sweater or put on a *cap*.
- Put on *sunglasses*.
- Slowly turn your head, stretching your neck and shoulder muscles.
- Put a small pillow on your desk and lay your head down on it.

Ears

- Put on a *hearing protection aid* or put in *ear plugs* (no more than twice a day for a maximum of half an hour).
- * Put in *ear plugs* for listening to *music*.
- Listen to *nature sounds* (sea, rain, birds, etc.).
- Listen to a story being read to you, by a teacher or a fellow student.
- What you, as a teacher, can do:
  - Tell rhymes, instead of a story.
  - Play a game where sounds must be identified. The students listen closely to the sounds happening in school and around it.
  - Turn a *metronome* to 60 beats per minute and let the students listen to this with their eyes closed. There are apps for the phone or tablet that have adjustable metronomes.

Mouth

- Chew specially made *chewing tools*.
- Chew a piece of *sugar free chewing gum*.

- Try to yawn.
* Drink water at a neutral temperature, through a *straw*.
- Close your eyes and calmly breathe into your lower abdomen. Breathe in through your nose, hold for three seconds and breathe out calmly through your mouth. Repeat this five to ten times.
- Put your hands on your stomach, close your eyes and breathe calmly. Ensure you can feel your belly expanding when you breathe in, and deflate when you breathe out. Breathe in through your nose, out through your mouth. Repeat this five to ten times.

Arms

- Put the palms of your hands together, fingers pointing up, and press them firmly against each other. See 'This is how you do it', below. Slowly build the pressure when you're doing this, and keep breathing.
- Push your hands on the desk (try to push the desk into the ground).
- Push yourself up slowly (put your hands on the seat of your chair, lift your feet off the ground and push, so your bottom doesn't touch the seat).
- Try to lift your chair by its seat, while sitting on it.
- Massage your own shoulders, the right shoulder with your left hand and vice versa.
- Let a classmate calmly massage your shoulders. Tell them if you want it to be done more firmly, less firmly, slower or faster.
- Calmly rub your skin and your clothes.
* Put a *big shawl* around your shoulders and upper arms and pull it tightly around yourself.

Legs

- Stretch your legs in front of you and slowly rub your hands up and down from your upper legs to your shins or feet.
- Stretch your legs as far as you can and wiggle your feet up and down, as if you are treading water.
- Put your feet up with your toes on the ground and shake your legs.

Posture

- Rock your body back and forth.

* Turn your chair around and sit down, straddling the chair, with your belly against the back of the chair. Cross your arms on the back of the chair and rest your head on your arms.

Other
- Put on something warm or pull a blanket around yourself.
- Work in a quiet place in the classroom (for example, using a *privacy shield*).
- Quietly count back from ten to one. Or from a higher number, if necessary.

This is how you do it
Put the palms of your hands together, fingers pointing up. Press your hands together for ten seconds, breathing continuously (this is, in most cases, an instruction everybody really needs). Let go for two seconds, then repeat.

This technique can be applied to be both activating and calming. See the explanation on activating and calming executions in Chapter 4.

Next to your chair
The following strategies can be executed by the student while standing next to their chair. These, too, are quick and easy to execute, and particularly suited to be executed by the whole class. For instance, when attention is fading during an exercise in comprehensive listening (activating) or when there is too much noise and excitement (calming).

The student can execute these strategies next to their chair during independent working time as well, because there are several strategies that involve little noise.

These strategies offer the *underresponsive* student the possibility to move more vigorously than when they remain seated.

> *Our most popular tip is: work standing up!*

Activate next to your chair

Little space for movement needed

- * Work standing up, at an elevated work surface; this can also be a cabinet or windowsill.
- • Stand up and drop yourself in your chair.
- * Stretch, making yourself as tall as possible (try touching the ceiling).
- • Give your lungs some space: breathe in deeply while you stretch your arms up and move them backwards (to give your chest as much space as possible) and breathe out while bringing your arms down again.
- • Gently shake your arms, legs and head.
- • Balance on one leg first, then the other (with or without your hands on your back or your head).
- • Everybody stand up and sing a song.
- • Wave.
- • Clap your hands. Mimic the rhythm of the teacher or a classmate.
- • Do repetition exercises, such as multiplication tables, while standing up and possibly while marching.
- • Stand up while listening to an explanation or when the teacher is reading to the class; you can shift from your toes to your heels, but do stay in the same spot.

More space for movement needed

- • Mirror a classmate: stand in front of each other and mirror each other's movements. Do this as fluently as possible, so it is unclear who starts and who follows.

- – Alternate between performing a movement for the other student to copy and copying the other student's movement.
- Bend forwards to touch the ground; try keeping your knees extended.
- Bend forward, with your head between your legs.
- Stand next to your chair and successively tap:
  - – your right hand on your left knee
  - – your left hand on your right knee
  - – your right hand on your left foot, along the front
  - – your left hand on your right foot, along the front
  - – your right hand on your left foot, along the back
  - – your left hand on your right foot, along the back
  - – and start again from the beginning.
- Jump up and down on the spot:
  - – with your hands in the air
  - – try and touch the ceiling
  - – jump low
  - – do jumping jacks.

- * Stamp your feet on the spot (providing this isn't a nuisance to other classes).
- March on the spot, lifting your knees as high as you can.
- Run on the spot.
- Dance on the spot, to music, if possible.
- Sing and participate in a 'movement song', such as 'head-shoulders-knees-and-toes'.

Sometimes it's nice for the student to get out of their chair for a bit to calm down. For example, when *overresponsivity* has caused so much tension to accumulate, it's nice to get rid of that tension through big movements.

Calming next to your chair
Little space needed

* Lie on your back, with your legs up against the desk or on your chair.
• Stretch, using slow movements. For example:
    – put one leg on your chair and bend forward towards your toes
    – grab your hands behind your back and extend and flex your back.

• Rock from left to right and forwards and backwards.
• Move your hands in big circles (slowly turning the steering wheel).
• Slowly point from the ceiling to the wall and then the floor.
• Slowly draw figures (such as geometric or fantasy shapes, letters or numbers) in the air, in front of you or on the ceiling. You can alternate between using your left and your right hand or use them simultaneously.
• Stand up straight, your arms relaxed next to your body and your eyes closed. Focus on your breathing. Breathe in slowly, into your lower abdomen, hold for three seconds and breathe out slowly through your mouth. Repeat this five to ten times.
• Stand up straight, your arms relaxed next to your body and your eyes closed. Focus on your body. First your feet, then your lower legs, your knees and upwards through your entire body. Breathe in deeply, once, then breathe out calmly. Open your eyes and sit down.
• Stand up straight, your arms relaxed next to your body and your eyes closed. Push your arms into your body as hard as you can, hold for three seconds and let go. Pull your shoulders up as high as you can, hold for three seconds and let go.

More space needed

- Slowly draw figures in the air, starting out really big, then slowly making them smaller, until they are as small as you can draw them.
- Let your upper body hang forwards (bend forwards at the hips, let your arms hang down).
* Sit down on the ground, pull your knees up, wrap your arms around your legs and pull your legs towards your body as tightly as you can.

- Stand up and spread your arms to the side, look over your right hand. Breathe in deeply, into your lower abdomen. When breathing out, turn to your right, as far as you can. See what point on the wall your fingers are pointing to. Turn back and repeat. Are you getting past the point on the wall you reached before? Repeat to the left.

In the classroom

For these strategies, the students will need more space. They're very appropriate for times when students have been sitting still for a while and there is no break or gym class coming up. A few strategies are more suitable for the *underresponsive* student who needs more movement than others. This student can be sent to do chores, for instance. You can also use the whole classroom to offer everyone a chance to catch their breath, for example when they've just had an intense lesson or a test, or as a strategy preceding an exciting event.

It can also be nice for the *underresponsive* student to get away from their spot completely and be allowed to move around the entire classroom. Being able to make big movements provides them with the opportunity to regain their alertness.

Activating in the classroom
Individual

- Do chores that require moving around:
  - take the chairs off the tables
  - hand out materials

- – wipe the chalkboard or whiteboard clean
- – water the plants (using a *watering can* filled all the way up, because that will be heavy, which has an activating effect)
- – sweep (a part of) the classroom with a *broom*.
- Wash your hands using cold water.
- Stand on a *balance board* while answering the teacher's questions.
- Walk around while trying to solve a problem.

For the whole class

* Perform a call and response song.

- Do the crab-walk without touching other students (walking sideways on hands and feet, while your bottom is pointing to the floor).
- March through the classroom, without touching people or things.
- Lie on your back, knees bent, feet flat on the floor. Make a bridge by lifting your bottom as high as you can.

- Turn around in circles on your bottom: sit on the floor with your arms wrapped around your knees and make circles, without falling over.

- Jump around the classroom (can also be done with frog jumps).
- Crawl around the classroom.
- Dance to *music*.
- Listen (or dance) to activating *music* such as dance or house music or rock 'n' roll.
* Push with stretched arms:
  - – against a wall or windowsill; trying to make the classroom 'bigger'
  - – against a classmate's hands. See 'This is how you do it', below.

- Walk around in circles through the classroom without touching things or people.
- Play 'patty cake' or other clapping games or songs.
- Do the 'coffee grinder': put one arm on the floor, stretched, put your feet as far away from your arm as you can and now walk around your arm in a circle.

- Sit down in front of a fellow student, legs wide, feet touching each other. Grab each other's wrists and move forwards and backwards as far as you can ('rowing').

This is how you do it

Have students stand in front of each other and have them put their hands flat against each other. The goal is for them to push each other's hands as hard as they can, without the other falling over. When one of the students says 'stop', both will (calmly) stop pushing.

There are fewer options that utilize the entire classroom for calming down. Moving around the classroom can easily lead to activation. This is because of all the obstacles in the classroom and all the students you might bump into. It's best to relax while sitting down or standing still, or walking around outside the classroom.

The *overresponsive* student can do their own, personal chores; chores that don't require them to walk around a lot, but that offer them the possibility to find a quiet place.

Calming in the classroom
Individual

- Do calming chores:
  - sharpen pencils

- – staple papers together (preferably slightly bigger piles of paper)
- – use a *hole puncher* to punch holes in paper (preferably slightly bigger piles of paper)
- – clean the *fish tank*.
* Watch the *fish* in the *fish tank* (this can also be done on a screen).
• Count (or look at) the shoes of everyone in the classroom.
• Retreat to a corner, for example with a bean bag or big box to sit in.

For the whole class

• Put on calming *music* (slow tempo) and listen to it. Look for a space in the classroom that feels comfortable, or stay in your chair.
* Walk through the classroom in slow motion, touching nothing and nobody.
• What you, as a teacher, can do:
  – Let students find their own spot in the classroom where they can comfortably sit, stand or lie down. Have them close their eyes and read a relaxing visualization ('Imagine you are lying on a blanket in the sun, you hear the birds sing softly...'). Use a book, podcast or other source that has visualizations for children. Search words are 'visualizations', 'relaxation' and 'guided meditation'. You might include the word 'children'.
  – Use yoga exercises for children. There are many examples available online.

6

Strategies Outside the Classroom

What's this chapter about?

In this chapter, we provide strategies for situations outside the classroom, for example in the hallway or in PE lessons. We also look at situations in the playground and during school gatherings. Furthermore, we provide strategies for when you are out and about, such as on a school trip, on the bus to swimming lessons or during an excursion.

Activating and calming

One student may need extra input, whereas another may need input removed. Therefore, we have categorized the strategies as activating and calming. Activating is to be used for the underresponsive student, calming for the overresponsive student.

- Some of the calming strategies are meant for blowing off steam, for example by moving or fiddling with something. Assessing what the student needs can be done with the help of the SPI-viewing guide in Chapter 4.
- Some strategies can be executed in both an activating and a calming manner. Revisit the section in Chapter 4, 'At what pace should a strategy be executed?' This explains how certain strategies can have both an activating and calming effect.
- A few strategies will be further explained in Chapter 7. There, we will explain why some strategies are activating or calming, tell you more about tools and provide information from scientific studies concerning some of the strategies.

Notes

- When 'you' is used in the strategies, it refers to the student. You, the teacher, provide instruction and demonstrate the exercise.
- In the exercises, you will see that some words are *italicized*. This indicates mention of tools that aren't general household items and should therefore be organized before starting.

Four types

For each part, we first look at the individual situation. We explain what the differences with the situation in the classroom are. Then, examples of reactions from the underresponsive and overresponsive student are discussed. The examples are somewhat exaggerated, so it's easier to recognize the type of student. Once again, we distinguish four types of student, as they appear in the SPI-viewing guide.

- Actively underresponsive (needs extra input and looks for it).
- Passively underresponsive (needs extra input and *doesn't* look for it).
- Actively overresponsive (is bothered by input and avoids it).
- Passively overresponsive (is bothered by input and *doesn't* avoid it).

Leaving the classroom
Situation
When you move from one space to another with your students, a lot needs to be done. Everyone needs to:

- hear what is going to happen, where, how long it will take and so on
- clean up their things

- bring the right things
- bring their coat and/or bag
- leave the room
- stand in a line
- walk away at the same time.

Behaviour

The *underresponsive* student has difficulty following instructions and performing all those actions. They do not get the instructions very well and are less aware of what is required of them. They don't receive all the information. This student can be overly active in order to experience more input (active). But they can also be a bit sluggish, for example they get in the way (passive).

Activating while changing locations

- Give the student a task, a responsibility, that is linked to (the transition to) the next activity. The task provides focus, which helps alertness. For instance:
  - carrying part of the required materials
  - holding doors open
  - counting classmates and reporting whether everyone is there.
- Pair the student who absorbs less information with a student who knows what needs to be done.
- Give the student something in their hands to fiddle with.
- Have the student jump up and down five times before you leave.
- Let the student lead the way, keep the doors open for everyone and then race-walk to the front again (limit disturbance by having them do this in silence).
- Let the student run up and down the stairs before walking along.
- Have the student walk hand in hand with another student.
- Give the student a place in the middle of the line or group, so they receive sensory input from classmates all around them, in terms of sounds, movement and touch.

The *overresponsive* student has problems with changing environments. Unfamiliar input is introduced, which requires a lot of attention. The student mainly wants to keep their distance from others and is not flexible (active), or they are irritated and therefore snappy and easily angered (passive).

Calming while changing locations

- Give the student things to carry; the weight has a calming effect:
  - a stack of books for the library
  - PE equipment
  - materials that will be used in the other room.
- Give the student something they can fiddle with in their hands.
- Prepare the overresponsive student in good time if the transition is an exception, so they know what to expect as much as possible. Let them know when they will return to the familiar schedule, to the routine.
- Also announce scheduled activities that require changing location, for example: 'In 15 minutes we will go to the PE hall.'
- See if it is possible for a student who is upset every morning because of the hustle and bustle in the corridor to enter the room first or last in the morning, when everyone is already sitting and the corridors are almost empty.
- Have the student take their coat and bag first or last, so they do not end up in the crowd when everyone is grabbing their coat and bag.
- Have the student hang their coat on the side of the coat rack in an easily accessible place.
- Have the student join the line last, so that there is no hustle behind them, they have a good overview and the chances of being touched unexpectedly are lower.
- If possible, avoid busy moments in the corridor, or let the overresponsive student go into the corridor before or after a busy moment.
- Give the overresponsive student the choice whether to walk hand in hand.
- Have the student put on a cap or hoody when they are in the corridor.

In the changing room
Situation

It is usually noisy in the changing room. There is an excited atmosphere and people are talking and laughing out loud.

The *underresponsive* student will feel fine because of this, because they experience more input. They are having fun and are getting dressed (active). If there still isn't enough input to activate them, their thoughts will wander and getting dressed will go slower (passive).

Activating in the dressing room

- Make sure the student is standing up while changing clothes, instead of sitting down.
- Ask the student to take off their shoes and socks first so feeling the cool floor can activate them. Have them put on their trainers last.
- Connect the student with a classmate and have them improve their 'personal changing record'. In silence. Let the partner count silently or use a *stopwatch*.
- Keep (extra) PE clothing at school if the student often forgets to bring it from home.
- Attach a list to the PE bag with everything it needs to contain.
- If possible, talk to the student, ask questions, make jokes.

Behaviour

The *overresponsive* student will mostly be bothered by the proximity of others and by smells, movements and sounds. They will try to claim their own space, as far away from others as possible (active). The smaller and noisier the dressing room is, the tenser this student will get, and they might become withdrawn or angry. This student is in survival mode and is therefore unable to communicate properly (passive).

Calming in the dressing room

- Provide this student with a quiet place in the dressing room.
- Let the student create a routine, so they always

put on their clothes in the same order. They could put this order on a laminated card to hang on their PE bag. This could say:
  - Take off coat and shoes. Hang up coat.
  - Take off and hang up trousers and shirt.
  - Put on PE bottoms.
  - Put on PE shirt.
  - Put on trainers.

The back of the card could show the order for getting dressed after PE class.

- Have the student use hearing protection (e.g. *ear defenders*) in the dressing room.
- Bring PE clothes that are easy to put on and take off. This will be less frustrating: bottoms with an elastic waistband; trainers with Velcro; a baggy T-shirt.
- This also applies to regular clothing. For example, clothing that's easily fastened and socks and shoes that can easily be taken off and put on.
- Put up long hair or wear it in a braid on PE days.

In the PE hall

Situation

The PE hall is a large space where students move, climb, run and throw balls. The atmosphere is exuberant; people talk louder than in the classroom.

For the *underresponsive* student, the PE hall is a space in which they look for sensory input and where they can move around freely. They can be clumsy sometimes, and bump into classmates and PE equipment. Bumping into people and things can also occur because it's nice to get more sensory input, just like when they are running or walking on their toes (active). The underresponsive student who is less easily engaged in the lesson may be sitting or standing a bit slouched and may not be absorbing all the instructions (passive).

Activating in PE

- Have the student do an activity that 'wakes up' their body before doing complex exercises or giving them longer instructions to process. For example:
  - sprinting
  - jumping jacks
  - swinging on the ropes or gymnastic rings
  - climbing
  - jumping on a small trampoline.
- Even while waiting for their turn, the student could occasionally do jumping jacks or sprints. Come to clear agreements about this, so it doesn't disturb the game or exercise.
- Have the student listen to instructions while standing up instead of sitting down (make sure they stay in the same place by indicating that

place, for example on a floor line or with a cross, dot or a mat). They can rock from their toes to their heels.
- Let the student help with the preparation, shifting or distribution of materials.
- Use a powerful voice and varying rhythm when giving individual instructions or encouragement.

Behaviour

For the *overresponsive* student, the PE hall is a turbulent place, full of relative chaos during games, with lots of sounds, movement and physical contact with classmates. For this student, movement has a calming effect, it gives them an opportunity to get rid of the tension that has accumulated because of overresponsivity. They will defend their personal space through clear instructions and signals to others, verbally and physically (active). They might also start grumbling and get angry or start crying because they are scared (passive).

Calming in PE

- Give the student space:
  - let them sit or stand on the sidelines
  - let them go first or last (discuss this with the student so they know why they are 'always the first or last')
  - with the busier games you can see if there is a task for the student on the sidelines of the game. Refereeing, counting exercises or keeping time are just a few suggestions. This way, they can participate, but without getting completely overstimulated.

- Respect that the overresponsive student may be anxious to have their feet off the floor and can be fearful when climbing.
- Use a calm voice when giving individual instructions or encouragement. Enthusiastic encouragement can be far too much in terms of sensory input, causing the student to become overwhelmed.
- Running laps can help eliminate the frustration and irritation of overresponsivity.
- If necessary, have the overresponsive student relax in a quiet corner.

In the playground
Situation
The playground is a space with a lot of freedom. There is less direct supervision than in the classroom and students can choose their own activities. There is a lot of noise and movement; the chances of being touched by fellow students are high.

Similarly to in the PE hall, the *underresponsive* student can come into their own in the playground, because there are many opportunities to get extra input. They are moving enthusiastically, sometimes being clumsy again and bumping into others (active). The underresponsive student who is not very active hangs around at the edge of the playground or isn't aware of all the rules of a game, possibly leading to them getting into a fight with fellow students (passive).

Activating in the playground

- If the student can't come up with ideas themselves, discuss with them what they can do:
  - build an insect house
  - write their name with twigs and leaves
  - use chalk to create a big drawing on the ground or on a wall (when making large drawings, the student moves more, which is activating)
  - participate in a game.
- Make sure the student spends enough time on the playground equipment, because movement will activate them.
- Use the playground outside of breaks as well:
  - allow the student to run a lap (for example, before doing a test)
  - have the student sweep the playground, along with other classmates who can use some exercise too.

- Consult with the clumsy student who often bumps into classmates, who then get angry as a result.
- Decide on a signal classmates can give when there is a collision. This way there won't be an argument and the student becomes more aware of their behaviour.
- Give the student an active role so they get more movement input. For example, they always go to retrieve the ball when it rolls off the field. Moving keeps them sharp.
- Make sure that the student keeps moving, even when they have to wait for a while or during quieter games such as marbles. Let them do jumping jacks, for example.

Behaviour

The *overresponsive* student won't be quick to get involved in the bustle, but will do their own thing. For example, they can hang around at the edge of the playground and chat with friends or walk around on their own. If they engage in play, they want it done their way (active). The overresponsive student can quickly become irritated during play due to the large amount of input. They forgot how much input there is during a game. So they join, but then stop after four minutes, dead tired from the sensory overload (passive).

Keep in mind that, for a seriously overresponsive student, playtime can be a moment to unwind as well. Overresponsive children can enjoy moments alone.

Calming in the playground

- Provide a space in the playground where there are no balls and where people do not run: for example, create a quiet place to sit in the playground.
- Offer materials for calmer and/or more individual play:
  - playing marbles provides an opportunity to play together without physical contact and bumping into each other
  - passing a ball around provides the same opportunity
  - skipping rope offers the possibility of blowing off steam. This can be done alone or together. If more than one student participates, the overresponsive student can turn the rope

- playing hopscotch can help with blowing off steam as well. Once again, this can be done alone or together, without physical contact
- bouncing a tennis ball off the wall can be done on your own, but also with others.
- Have the student wear a hearing protector or *earbuds* for listening to music.
- Allow the student to withdraw. Have the student relax in a quiet place during break. And perhaps more often than just during the scheduled breaks.

During gatherings
Situation
During gatherings – such as the Christmas celebration, a concert or a play – many children are together in a limited space. The students usually sit side by side on benches or close together on the floor. There is noise and excitement. Before the speech, play, choir or concert starts, students may be yelling and teachers are giving directions.

Gatherings are pleasant sources of input for the *underresponsive* student. They go along with the excitement, call out, point and laugh and may become a bit hyper. During the performance, especially if it takes a long time, they may have difficulty keeping their attention on the performance and start looking around and chatting with classmates (active). It may also be that the underresponsive student will just passively experience the happening: they are sitting a bit slouched and aren't absorbing all information (passive).

Activating during gatherings

- Take care that the student has a clear task to focus on; have them keep an eye on the time, for example.
- Give the student 'activating in your chair' strategies (see Chapter 5).

- Pair the student with a buddy who can point out to them when singing and clapping are allowed.
- Seat the student in a somewhat busier spot: next to the aisle or at the front. During the gathering there may be extra sensory input here, because people are still walking back and forth.
- At Christmas dinner or other food-based events, such as a joint breakfast:
  - put them next to an enthusiastic, chatting classmate
  - give the student the task of handing out things and arrange a route where they cannot easily knock something over
  - offer them crispy and strong-tasting food, so they have to chew a lot and can taste everything more intensely.

Behaviour

For the *overresponsive* student, gatherings are a 'waterfall of sensory input' that can cause a lot of stress. They will look for the quietest place (active). If this does not work and the student ends up in the middle of the bustle, it can lead to a quarrel, because the stress can make the student more irritable (passive).

Calming during gatherings

- In drama, when the student does not want to be the centre of attention (on the stage), a supporting task may be possible. For example, doing something with music, scenery or lighting. This way, the student can make their contribution without being overresponsive.

- Discuss with the student what the best place in the audience is:
  - next to a trusted classmate
  - next to the teacher
  - next to the aisle or right in the middle so no students have to pass in front of them
  - at the back, so they have a good overview.
- Bring hearing protection, so the student always has the option to use it.
- Have them put on clothing with a hood so they can put that up.
- Bring something for the student to fiddle with or chew on.
- If the student comes to the gathering, agree on what they can do when it gets too much for them:
  - Who do they tell when/if they leave?
  - Where will they go? For example, to the classroom, to the janitor, to the library? Make sure the people in those places know about this.
  - What will they do instead?
- At Christmas dinner or other food-based events, such as a joint breakfast:
  - Together with this student, find the quietest place, away from walking routes.
  - Sit them next to a quiet classmate.
  - Let them be the first or last to pick out their food at a buffet. Or, if they really prefer to stay in their seat, ask an (underresponsive) classmate to bring the food.
  - Have hearing protection at the ready.
  - Offer them food with a soft or smooth texture that is mild or sweet in taste, so they don't get too much sensory input in their mouth and taste more accessible flavours.

School parties

Situation

There are many people at a school party, a lot of movement, loud noises and flashing or bright lights.

This is a great environment for the *underresponsive* student. They get activated and can enjoy the spectacle from the sidelines or plunge themselves into the crowd on the dance floor. They can be a bit awkward when dancing, be too wild and bump into people (active). The underresponsive student can hang out at the side and not engage in the festivities (passive).

Activating during school parties

- Encourage the student to participate in the festivities such as dancing and chatting.

Behaviour

The *overresponsive* student experiences the school party as a place full of noise and movement. They can probably be found somewhere at the back, away from the speakers. Maybe they are standing near the cloakroom, where they hang around and chat with others (active). The overresponsive student who is in the middle of a crowd may not be so open to having a conversation; they are mainly busy surviving among all the intense input (passive).

Calming during school parties

- Bring hearing protection.
- Have the student dance among friends; they can make sure fellow students won't bump into them.
- Let them walk around outside every now and then, or retreat to a quiet place.
- Bring fidget toys that fit in their pocket.
- Make sure they arrive early, when it's not that busy yet. This way, the amount of sensory input builds up gradually. This means they won't suddenly be overcome by a lot of input, as can happen at the height of the party.
- Give them something to do on the sidelines during the party: picking the music, helping out in the cloakroom, pouring drinks.

On the street

Situation

When outside, you can be confronted with many different situations: quiet neighbourhoods or busy junctions, lots of traffic or not so much traffic, sunny weather, wind and rain. The students are walking two by two or in small groups. There is less direct supervision and a lot of distraction.

The street is a place full of extra input for the *underresponsive* student. For example, they might jump or run. This makes them more alert, but less able to pay attention to traffic (active). If they are not sufficiently alert, because not all input is processed, their behaviour is also not safe for traffic. For example, they do not see that the traffic light is red (passive).

Activating on the street

- Put the student somewhere in the middle of the group.
- Connect the student to an active classmate, who has a good overview of what needs to be done.
- Have the student – possibly together with a number of classmates – jump as high as they can a couple of times.
- Ask this student to sing songs with a few others (at times when that's possible in regards to road safety).
- Have the student take giant steps or little gnome steps.
- Have the student skip or walk on tiptoe.

Behaviour

When in traffic, the *overresponsive* student is more concerned with avoiding crowds and noises than with paying attention (active). They can also behave in an unsafe way, because they are flooded with sensory input and therefore lose sight of what is happening. They are so preoccupied with bothersome input that they stall at the pedestrian crossing or, the opposite, cross the road while a car is coming towards them. They no longer make well-considered decisions, because there is too much information (passive).

Calming on the street

- Have the student walk next to a trusted classmate.
- Give the student something to carry (helps them keep a grip literally and figuratively).
- Have the student be the last in line (with a chaperone behind them).
- Give the student the freedom to change places in the line (for example, when commotion occurs near to them).
- Respect that the student may not want to talk. They are busy processing enough input as it is.
- Make sure the student has something with them to fiddle with or chew on.

Transport (parents, public transport, coach)
Situation
When students are transported by coach or private car, there is often 'organized chaos' with a lot of noise, hustle and bustle, arranging who's to sit with whom, and excited or tired students, chaperones and teachers. When you travel on public transport, there is a lot of input as well. Especially on metro and train platforms, and at tram and bus stops; so much happens at the same time:

- There are many people.
- There are many – sometimes loud and unexpected – sounds.
- There is a lot of movement of people, vehicles and other objects, such as traffic lights changing colour.
- There is time pressure.
- People are looking for information on catching the right connection.
- People are looking for information on the correct departure times and places.

Behaviour
Activating the *underresponsive* student will be especially necessary when the student approaches the means of transport or has to leave it. The underresponsive student will not have a hard time keeping up to speed and paying attention; they have plenty of room to walk, run and bump into people/things (active). This student can be found in their seat in all kinds of positions, except sitting (active). The student can also – after sitting still on a seat for a while – become drowsy from riding the bus, car, tram or metro (passive). Once they are in their chair, activation is less important. If they are on the road, they do not have to pay attention unless instructions are given.

Activating during transport

- Give the student an active role:
  - let them count the students
  - give them things to hand out
  - give them the responsibility for material that must be brought along.
- Look at 'Activating on the street', above.

- Have the student look for certain landmarks (look out for a specific exit on the motorway) or let them count white cars for a while.

The *overresponsive* student lacks overview during this activity. They experience unexpected and new input as threatening. They will, where possible, look for relatively quiet corners (active). The student can freeze in very busy, unfamiliar situations. Or they might get into a quarrel with classmates whom they think are too wild and are making too much noise (passive).

Calming during transport

- Discuss with the student which spot is pleasant. For example, a window seat, next to a quiet student or a chaperone. They might want to be at the front of the bus for a good view of the road and route. Or perhaps all the way at the back, so they can oversee all movement in the bus.
- Tell the chaperone which input can be a problem for an overresponsive child, and that there can sometimes be strong reactions to, for example, an unexpected loud noise.
- Have the student (in public transport, together with a chaperone) be the first to get in and out.
- Make sure the student has one contact person.
- Make sure the student knows what is going to happen and when, so that they have a sense of control.
- Pair the student with a trusted classmate.
- Prepare the student for metro and train platforms, tram and bus stops, and discuss possible strategies:
  - link the student to someone who can keep an overview and who can make sure the student ends up in the right means of transport on time and gets out again
  - have the student stand or sit against a wall or billboard
  - let them put on their *hoody*
  - make sure the student stands a little further away from the track.
- Have the student wear a *hearing protector* or *earbuds* that allow them to listen to *music* to mask other sounds. This is only possible when the student does not have to pay attention to the traffic and listen to the traffic noises.

On a school trip/excursion
Situation
Many new, unexpected, exciting, fun and interesting things happen during school trips and excursions. But there are also times when you have to wait a long time.

The *underresponsive* student looks forward to the new, interesting and exciting input that comes their way during an outing. They watch and participate. Until there's a long wait. Then they might start to mess around, talk or play to get more input (active). Or they might become sleepy and not realize the waiting time is over and the group is moving on. Because there is no routine, the student may have difficulty giving the correct responses (passive).

Activating on a school trip/excursion

- Many unusual things happen on a school trip/excursion, and you are completely out of your routine. This alone is probably enough to activate the underresponsive student.
- Sometimes, it's necessary to wait a long time during a school trip. The underresponsive student isn't bothered by this. Should you want to activate them, give them a leading role in a game or song meant to make the waiting easier.
- Take fidget and chewing aids with you, in case activation is needed, for example while listening to a story during a tour.

Behaviour
The *overresponsive* student experiences this new, interesting and exciting input as unsafe. Again, they will search for quiet places (active) or they can be moody and stubborn (passive).

Calming on a school trip/excursion
- Discuss unfamiliar events in advance. Make an overview together concerning what, where, how, when, with whom, what to bring with you and why. For instance, a museum visit:
  - what: we are going to an exhibition about musical instruments, there we will get a tour by a museum employee and then we will be making music together
  - where: in the museum of indigenous cultures
  - how: we will walk through the park

- – when: we leave on Friday at 09:30 and will walk back to school at 12:30
  - – with whom: Years 2 and 3, two teachers and six parents
  - – what you should bring: your chewing necklace and your flute
  - – why: the outing is in the context of Mister Herman's music project in Years 2 and 3.
- Discuss what is familiar:
  - – their own teacher will come along
  - – the student will be going with their own class
  - – their best friend is in their group
  - – meals will be at the same time.
- Bring familiar things such as: their own lunch (if possible), a stuffed animal or their own pillow.
- Give the student something they can hold during the outing. Discuss with the student what qualifies. This can be a stuffed animal for the younger student. With an older student it can be a keychain or something with which they can fiddle and/or chew on.
- Make sure there is a quiet space on the way there and back.
- Schedule alone-time or time to rest.
- Do not ask the student to talk if they aren't doing this on their own. Processing all this new input already takes enough energy; having to communicate simultaneously will be too much.
- Make sure that, when there is a long period of waiting, the student has a quiet place where they can go to relax.
- Have the student use *earbuds* to listen to *music* of their choice.

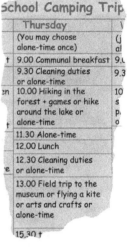

School Camping Trip

Thursday	
(You may choose alone-time once)	(j al
9.00 Communal breakfast	9.(
9.30 Cleaning duties or alone-time	9.3
10.00 Hiking in the forest + games or hike around the lake or alone-time	10 s p, o
11.30 Alone-time	
12.00 Lunch	
12.30 Cleaning duties or alone-time	
13.00 Field trip to the museum or flying a kite or arts and crafts or alone-time	
15.30 +	

Do not expect students to (be able to) process any other information if you have just told them that they are going on a school trip. Processing the excitement, or shock, requires all the attention of the brain. Don't even expect your answer to a question from the student – about the school trip – to be remembered. The excitement first has to abate and a feeling of security must return. Only then can the information you give them be processed in the right way, so it can be remembered. This process may need to be repeated several times, so don't be surprised if children ask about the same thing again (and again).

7

More about Strategies and Tools

What's this chapter about?

In this chapter, we explain how certain strategies work and we discuss tools you can use when executing them. At the end, we discuss scientific studies. These show that several strategies we mention have a positive effect on learning.

How do certain strategies work?

In previous chapters, several strategies are mentioned which are further explained below. We explain why the strategies work the way they do and what makes them successful. We do this as follows:

- We provide specific information about how the strategy or tool works.
- We indicate whether a strategy/aid is particularly suitable for underresponsive or overresponsive students, or for both.
- You read what the best time span is: how long do you use a strategy or tool for?
- You get tips to choose the right tool.
- You receive advice on what to look for when purchasing aids.

Strategy: Chewing

Chewing, sucking and sipping/nibbling help you regulate when you are feeling tense, but also when you are feeling sluggish. It is a widely used strategy. Everyone uses their mouths to regulate tension, for example by squeezing their lips together, chewing a pen, biting their nails or nibbling on a piece of liquorice. When you are underresponsive, chewing helps, because you use your muscles, which has an activating effect. When you are overresponsive, chewing acts as a kind of outlet; it reduces tension. By chewing, you can blow off steam and calm down.

Although chewing gum is often strictly forbidden in the classroom, it can be useful. Fortunately, there are many alternatives to chewing gum these days. Chewing aids exist in the form of necklaces, bracelets or key rings, or materials that can be put on the back of a pencil or thin pen which you can then chew or nibble on.

How long can you chew on something?

It is difficult to indicate how long it is benefi-
cial for a student to chew on something. If the
material is not harmful to the teeth, a student
can use chewing aids all day long. If in doubt
whether the child is chewing too much, the
parent can consult with their dentist. The
student who is using chewing materials for
the first time must build up the chewing time,
otherwise their jaw muscles will become sore.
The student who is used to chewing on something will no longer be bothered by this.

How do you choose the right chewing aids?

- The various aids that are available often state whether they are suitable for light, medium or heavy chewing needs. This has to do with the robustness of the material. A younger student can use the softer materials. The older and stronger the student is and the greater the need for chewing, the firmer the material must be.
- The student can see for themselves which tool they like. There are very attractive things available, in all sorts of colours and shapes, for all gender identifications and for different ages. *Note:* the nicer the material looks, the softer it often is. For these aids, a different raw material is used, which is easier to shape and pour.
- There are different options for storing the chewing aid. Some

tools fit in your pocket, others can be hooked onto a loop and used as a key ring, some can be tied on a string, and then there are some that can be worn around your wrist or neck.

Strategy: Deep pressure and movement input

This strategy is relatively unknown, and we will therefore explain it in more detail. The brain distinguishes two types of sensory input through the skin:

- Input which the brain classifies as external. With light pressure or light touch – for example, with tickling, very light friction or by touching little hairs – only the upper dermis is touched. Insects, spiders or scratchy twigs also cause light touch. This input triggers an alarm signal. External input can be harmful and, to the brain, resembles danger. That is why, with light touches, the alarm goes off relatively quickly and a defence response will follow.
- Input which the brain concludes comes from within. When you are touched calmly and very firmly, this input is detected in the deeper layers of the skin; that is why we call this 'deep pressure'. This input is also partially detected by receptors in the muscles and joints. The brain therefore believes that this input comes from within the body.

> *Deep pressure feels the same as movement input and that input is generally safe.*

Deep pressure feels the same as movement input and that input is generally safe. Deep pressure is therefore usually considered to be pleasant. You experience it when you feel a (heavy) weight on you or someone touches you firmly, when something is wrapped tightly around your body or when you get a massage. Heavy work, which requires the use of a lot of muscles, such as carrying something, pushing or pulling or exercising, also provides deep pressure.

Calmly applied deep pressure has a calming and positive effect on the brain's stress mechanism. In stressful situations, the input filter is wide open for all sensory input, which means that it's easier for you to be overresponsive. Deep pressure ensures this mechanism is weakened.

When deep pressure is applied quickly, irregularly and unexpectedly, it has an activating effect.

How long can you apply deep pressure for?

If the deep pressure input remains the same, the body gets used to the input and it loses its calming effect. Constant deep pressure input, for instance by not moving when using a weighted blanket, pressure vest (provides pressure by inflating the vest) or a weighted vest (provides pressure because it has little weights in it), will therefore stop working after about half an hour. So, wait at least an hour before reapplying the deep pressure and then again for only about half an hour. When the deep pressure input varies in pace, pressure and speed, it will continue to have an activating or calming effect, for example with firm rubbing, pushing or pulling and while exercising. Therefore, there is no time limit to this. As long as the student needs the calming effect of the deep pressure input, you can continue providing it.

How do you choose the right tool for deep pressure?

You don't do this yourself. These types of aids are fairly specific and are almost always selected with the help of a therapist who specializes in sensory processing. Make sure that you are advised by an occupational or physical therapist or speech therapist while trying out these tools. They will tell you about slowly increasing the use of the tool, how much weight to use, how long you can use the tool and what to expect. For example, in the classroom a weighted stuffed animal, weighted cushion, pressure vest or weighted vest can be used.

Strategy: Carry something during a change in activities

By letting the student carry something in their hands, you literally and figuratively help them get a grip during a change in activities. This helps the underresponsive student focus – they have to stay focused or they will drop something. This focus has an activating effect, which increases their alertness. A stack of books or a box or crate with gym items has a calming effect, due to the weight, which is pleasant for the overresponsive student. This student could also carry a backpack with extra weight; this provides deep pressure, which is calming.

How long can you carry something for?

You can carry something for as long as it takes to change activities and you don't need your hands for anything else. You can wear a weighted backpack for as long as it is pleasant and convenient to do so. The strategy works as long as you're carrying something. Because you are moving, the body doesn't get used to the extra input of the weight and the strategy will be effective.

It isn't always safe to carry something in your hands. The teacher can therefore place a backpack in the classroom to use during a change of activities. This can be used to transport books or other materials, so that the student's hands are free to open doors or safely walk up and down stairs.

Strategy: Fiddling

Fiddling feels good. Everyone does it sometimes, for example during a meeting, while watching TV or during a telephone conversation. People also like holding something during a discussion. It is nice to move your fingers and to have a grip on something in a certain way by holding onto something or by drawing. This way you can keep your head in the game (activating) or relieve tension (calming).

Fiddling is mentioned with both activating and calming strategies. When you are underresponsive, fiddling provides your body with extra input, which has an activating effect. The student who needs this extra input will often pull and push the fiddling tool harder to receive input. The student who is overresponsive can use fiddling to divert their attention away from disturbing input or to relieve tension. This is how fiddling helps them calm down.

How long can you fiddle for?

You can hold something in your hands to fiddle with during a change of activities, when listening is needed for a long time and while reading. Really, any time the hands are free, and the student needs an activating or calming strategy. Because you constantly move your fingers in a different way, the body does not get used to this input and it remains effective. Therefore, there is no maximum amount of time for this strategy; fiddling can be done any time and anywhere.

How do you choose the right fiddling tool?

Use tools that make little noise and aren't too interesting, so that they don't distract the student (and others). Look at what the student is already using themselves as well. Pretty much everyone carries fiddling material with them. After all, you can fiddle with your hair, your face, your clothing, your jewellery, your glasses and so on. But you can also use other tools. To use them in the classroom, it is best if the tools don't make any noise and do not distract other students. Due to hygiene, you will only want to use washable materials for multiple people. When a student wears out a lot of tools, you can explain to parents what the purpose of the tools is and ask them if they can have their child bring specific things to school. Possibilities include:

- *Pieces of string* or *shoelaces*. You can fiddle with these endlessly and you can tie little knots in them, which you can then also fiddle with.
- *Velcro*. You can stick the soft side on a drawer or on the bottom of your desk. The student can rub this with their fingers.
- *Rubber band*, thin or thick. You can endlessly wrap this around your fingers and take it off again. Hair ties are nice, because they have a protective layer, so they are less likely to cut off circulation. Perhaps the rule will be needed that launching them at something or someone isn't allowed...
- *Kneaded eraser.* Good for squeezing, rolling and making all kinds of shapes.
- *Putty.* A kind of kneaded eraser, but much larger, that can be shaped indefinitely, available in different levels of resistance.
- *Rubber (stress) balls.* These come in all sizes and shapes.
- *Jewellery.* Necklaces, bracelets and earrings are great for fiddling with. However, it is nice when this can be done soundlessly.
- *Cords.* The cords of a hoody, cardigan or other clothing are fine for fiddling with.
- *Massage ball.* A rubber ball with soft spikes. Pleasant to roll back and forth in your hands and to squeeze.

- *Koosh ball.* A ball with rubber 'hairs', to feel, to pull and to wiggle back and forth.
- *Paper clip.* You can bend it, feel it and thread them together.
- *Tangle fidget toy.* You can keep twisting a Tangle; it consists of a number of parts that are connected to each other and that can move relative to each other. Tangles are available in various sizes, colours and textures, such as smooth, ribbed, rubbery and with round studs.

Strategy: Work standing up

You can perform writing and reading tasks while standing up, at a standing desk or high table, cupboard, wide windowsill or shelf at elbow height. Standing requires more muscle activity, which is activating, so a student can stay focused. This allows them to perform their schoolwork (listening, reading, writing) properly.

- A student with a limp, slouchy sitting posture often shows better handwriting when they write standing up. Because they are standing up, more muscles are at work in their trunk. This results in a good basis for shoulder and arm mobility.
- If a student has difficulty focusing on reading a book for a long time, they can keep it up longer when they are standing up.
- When the student needs to listen for a long time, they will drift off less quickly when they can stand (occasionally) while listening.
- When standing up, it's easier for a student to use their breath when reading out loud. It is easier to keep your trunk straight when standing up, which results in more space for your lungs.

When you have multiple tasks to perform standing up, you can have the student stand on a carpet tile or something similar, to define their spot.

The carpet tile indicates that moving around isn't the intention; this stops the student from wandering around. If they require even more activating input, they can rock from their toes to their heels or from one leg to the other.

How long can you work while standing?

How long they want to and can work standing up will be different for every student. It is nice to be able to alternate. When you choose to purchase a standing desk with a high chair, the student always has the choice between working while standing or sitting. When they have their own desk where both positions are possible – sitting and standing – the student can stay in the same place in the room if they want to change position. This ensures that standing up doesn't become ineffective. Because you are changing position, the input varies and so the brain doesn't adjust to it and continues to focus.

How do you choose the right standing desk?

Consider the following:

- Is the desk adjustable in height so you can use it for different students in successive years?
- Can the height be adjusted quickly? If so, you can use it for different students. This is convenient when there is a limited number of standing spaces in your classroom and multiple students want to use it.
- Is there sufficient storage space for school supplies? This is important if the student will always be working at the standing desk.

Strategy: Wobble cushion

It can be difficult for an underresponsive student to sit still. They need activating, new input and they get this by moving, for example by rocking their chair. However, rocking a chair can be disruptive, which is why you might use a wobble cushion. A wobble cushion is a cushion you put on the seat of a chair. Thanks to the cushion, the student needs to create less movement in order to feel comfortable and stay focused. The student's muscles are constantly active due to the wobble cushion. This way, the body constantly receives new input and it must continuously adapt to a new situation. There is extra alertness and therefore better concentration.

How long can you sit on a wobble cushion?

Use the wobble cushion for tasks where the student has to sit still for a relatively long time, which they aren't very good at. The cushion has the most effect when you use it for periods of around 30 minutes. When the student sits on the wobble cushion for longer, their body gets used to the extra movement input and it no longer helps with concentration. The student might even start to move more vigorously to still get that extra input.

How do you choose the right wobble cushion?

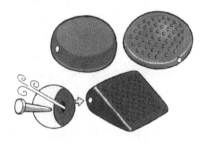

- There are thinner and thicker cushions, smooth cushions and cushions with soft spikes which provide extra sensory input. In any case, ensure that the student can reach the floor with their feet while sitting on the cushion. If necessary, use a lower chair or a footstool for this.
- Consider a cushion for which the level of inflation can be altered, as it can then be adjusted to the preference of the student. The more air, the more stable the cushion becomes.

Strategy: Balance board

A balance board is a board you stand and balance on. It is an activating strategy that can be used as a movement 'snack', but also during rote learning, such as multiplication tables.

How long should you stand on a balance board?

As long as it takes to do the activity for which you want to be extra alert, such as answering questions or rote learning. This usually means that you will stand on the wobble board for two to five minutes. It can also be longer, if there is time. The student does not get used to the input from the balance board, because they are constantly moving.

What should you look for when choosing a balance board?

- Make sure the balance board won't damage the floor. Place it on a piece of carpet if the bottom of the balance board might scratch the floor.
- Make sure the student is close to a wall or table, so they can put their hand against it or on it when they feel they are about to lose their balance.

Strategy: Drinking in the classroom

In many classes it is already permitted to drink water when you need it. Simply drinking a sip of water works very well to regulate alertness. Drinking cold water is activating, as is drinking water with lime, lemon and/or mint. Drinking water that is about room temperature has a calming effect, just like sucking through a straw.

How often should you drink water?

You can drink water whenever you need to be activated or calmed down. Every student can bring their own water bottle, which they place on their desk. This way, they will always have water at hand. The student who feels the need to take a little walk can go to refill the bottle, which means they will also have cooler water, directly from the tap. A few sips should be sufficient to have an effect.

What should you look for regarding water bottles?

The following points are good to consider:

- For the student who needs calming, the best option is to choose a water bottle with a straw or a sipper bottle.

- Make sure the bottles are easy to clean. The student who needs activation can be given the task of washing all bottles regularly.

Strategy: Hearing protection

Hearing protection has a calming effect on an overresponsive student. A hearing protector suppresses noise, which means you are less bothered by environmental noise.

Use hearing protection, for example, during independent work, while the teacher gives instructions to others or is talking to other students. Hearing protection can also be useful at meetings, in the playground or during excursions. A student may find it scary to put on a hearing protector because they do not feel safe when they cannot hear all the sounds. A solution for this is that the student sits down in a spot where they have a good overview of the space. This way they can see if something unsafe is happening.

How long can you wear hearing protection?

Hearing protection must be used very purposefully. You have to be careful not to overuse it. When you wear hearing protection throughout the day, your brain will increase sound sensitivity to compensate for the lack of information. Your brain tries to listen even better, in order to get information through the ears. This is counterproductive, because it makes the overresponsivity even worse. If a student often wants to shield themselves from (ambient) sounds, it will be better to use music, through earbuds, as we explain in the following strategy. Do not use hearing protection more than twice a day for a maximum of half an hour at a time.

> *It is possible to use a tool too much.*

How do you choose the right hearing protection?
There are many different hearing protectors on the market:

- earmuffs for adults and for children, with and without a filter
- earplugs made of foam, silicone or acrylic
- universal and custom-made earplugs.

The advantage of the large hearing protector, with earmuffs, is that it also provides deep pressure to the head, which can have a calming effect. When a student benefits from hearing protection a lot, but would rather not have anything on their head, you can discuss with the parent if they can buy customized hearing protection. This is a good alternative to a hearing protector with earmuffs, but more expensive. This is partly because it has to be refitted when the student grows.

It is practical to have a number of hearing protectors with earmuffs in the classroom, to be used by different students. Hearing protectors that are worn in the ears cannot be exchanged for hygiene reasons.

Strategy: Music carriers (iPod, MP3 player or smartphone)
To be less bothered by ambient noises (other students talking, construction work, noise in the room next door and the like), you can have the student use a music carrier. The student will use this to play music they like. It must be music that is well known to them and that is not distracting. This has a calming effect. For the student who needs extra input, listening to music while working independently can help. This can give the extra input they need to be activated.

How long can you listen to music?

As long as the activity lasts and as long as the music supports the student in doing their work.

How do you choose the right music?

The teacher doesn't have to do this. As long as it is music that isn't distracting. The student chooses their music themselves, so they have control over the type of sound they receive the strongest. They can't control ambient sounds, which means those sounds are more likely to distract them. Ambient sounds will more quickly receive the 'interesting' stamp. You can filter out your own chosen sounds more easily, which means you can focus on a different task. Therefore, the student must choose music that is so familiar that it will not distract them. When they are in a busy environment – for example, on the road during an excursion – and the goal is to isolate themselves from the crowds, they can choose music that is indeed distracting them. It should be music they really like, so their brain enjoys listening to this exciting input. The volume should not be too high; listening to anything above 80 dB (decibels) for an extended period causes hearing damage. It's about masking the ambient noise; you don't have to top their volume.

Strategy: Tennis balls or chair glides on the chair legs

Some chairs can cause annoying, scraping sounds. If there are students who are so bothered by this that they are startled every time and get a little stressed out by it, it's good to get rid of this. The overresponsive student will be grateful for this calming strategy. You can use tennis balls or chair glides to prevent the scraping sound. It's better not to use stick-on felt chair glides; they come off easily.

What should you pay attention to when purchasing chair glides?

Make sure that they not only prevent noise, but also don't leave marks on the floor. At a tennis club or through the internet you might be able to get a batch of rejected tennis balls for free or very little money, especially when you explain the good purpose they will serve! Cut an opening in the tennis balls with a knife and then stick the balls to the chair legs. You can also purchase chair glides, which are available in many shapes and sizes.

Strategy: Privacy shields

If a student is easily distracted by what they can see and hear around them, you can block the view from their workplace. There are different ways to apply this calming strategy. You can create a space behind a cupboard, in the corridor or in a corner of the room where there is little walking and fuss. If the student should stay in their own spot, you can work with screens or privacy shields. Or you can create a special 'silence spot' in the room using these screens and dividers. You can also do this with the help of a curtain. A cheap option is to screw the corner of a shower rail to the ceiling or the wall. Hang a curtain on this and you have a perfectly fine room separator.

How long do you use a privacy shield?

As long as the work lasts for which the student needs to be shielded from sensory input.

How do you choose the right privacy shield?

Privacy shields come in the form of large partitions to put on the floor and portable screens that are foldable. You can also make something yourself, using sturdy cardboard. Consider whether you want to create permanent places where the partitions can stay. Use a portable version when the screen has to stand on the student's desk. Points of focus are:

- Pay attention to the weight. There are lightweight screens, for example made from recycled jeans or sustainable plastic, and there are also wooden screens, which are slightly heavier.
- Pay attention to the thickness of the screen when it's folded. Does that thickness fit in the space you want to use to store the screen?
- Some screens have a built-in work surface; if this is the case, you must empty the desk before you can place the screen on it.
- Other screens only have three 'walls'; you can put this type on the desk without having to clear it first.

Strategies and science

The strategies discussed in this book are tried and tested and have been shown to have a positive effect on students' ability to focus on their work. In this section, we discuss some of the research that has been done which demonstrates their effectiveness.

Science about chewing

Although chewing gum is often strictly forbidden in the classroom, it could be very useful in maintaining alertness when students have to concentrate on a task for a long time (Morgan, Johnson and Miles, 2014).

Allen, Jacob and Smith (2014) also discovered that chewing gum increases alertness. They observed this effect during and immediately after chewing.

Science about movement and learning

A study conducted by the University of Groningen (Mullender-Wijnsma *et al.*, 2016) showed that children learn better when they move. The students who participated in the 'Fit and Vaardig' lessons (during which they were physically active while learning) achieved a learning gain of four months for maths and spelling within two years, compared with the control group.

The importance of recess was investigated at a school where they normally did not set aside time for playing. Forty-four children were allowed to have recess once a week. Their behaviour that day was compared with their behaviour on the days without recess. Specific attention was paid to work, mobility/restlessness and lethargy. A clear difference was observed, with 60 percent of the children on recess days being more task-oriented and less restless/mobile. There was no difference in effect between boys and girls (Jarrett *et al.*, 1998).

A research group of eight- to 11-year-olds was judged on their posture while receiving instructions. First, the students' working posture was observed without them having done activating exercises. This was compared with their working posture after they had done activating exercises. The research group was compared with a control group which did not receive activating exercises, to assess whether there was a difference in the amount of physical activity. Work attitude improved significantly in the research group (this means that a difference of more than 5 percent was perceived). On average, the improvement in work attitude was 8 percent and the group of children who previously scored the worst work attitude showed an improvement of 20 percent. An improvement in work attitude meant that the students were more focused on the instructions, rather than being busy with other things, unrelated to the instructions (Mahar *et al.*, 2006).

Doing short, moderately intensive exercises in the classroom during the school day seems to be effective in increasing alertness and thereby learning efficiency (Drolette *et al.*, 2014).

In a meta-study, 59 studies were analysed, about the effects of physical activity of children on their school performance. The results of the analysis showed a significant and positive effect. This study focused on general physical activities, not specifically in the classroom (Fedewa and Ahn, 2011).

In another study, 44 studies were analysed, about the effects of children's physical activity on their school performance. Here, too, the result was that physical activity improves cognitive development in children (Sibley and Etnier, 2003).

Playing a video game involving active physical movement, as opposed to a video game not involving physical moment, improved the response time and accuracy in children in an activity that was performed immediately afterwards (Best, 2012).

Science about fiddling

In a study where people had to listen to a monotonously recorded telephone message, it became clear that people who had been sketching/drawing while listening had retained 29 percent more of the content of the message (Andrade, 2010).

Behaviour such as scratching, biting your lip and touching your face is also considered fiddling and has been studied to see how it helps to deal with feelings of stress. This study showed that this kind of behaviour helps regulate stress (Mohiyeddini and Semple, 2013).

In another study, fiddling was associated with alertness. Fiddling turned out to be a very good indicator that people in a lecture needed a break or a change of pace because they could no longer focus sufficiently. In addition, fiddling contributed significantly to remembering information (Farley, Evan and Kingstone, 2013).

Science about working standing up in school

There has not been much research into the use of standing desks in schools. Working while standing up on a large scale in school is a relatively new phenomenon. The reason for using standing desks lies in improving health by sitting less and exercising more. More research has been conducted with adults at work. Here, too, particular attention was paid to ergonomics and the effects on muscles and joints.

A study on active workplaces looked at 32 studies, ten of which were among schoolchildren. A positive result was observed for the health and activity of the students. Regarding cognitive development and productivity, more research is needed (Torbeyns et al., 2014).

A small study looked at the impact on schoolchildren of working at a standing desk with a high stool. The children and teachers were enthusiastic about working while standing up, because of the flexibility it provides. The cautious conclusion of this study is that standing desks can be used well in a classroom and that their use reduces the number of hours in which children choose to sit (Hinckson et al., 2013).

In another small study, two classes from different schools were compared. In one school, children sat in their chairs 97 percent of the time, a third of the time sitting bent over at an angle of over 45°. In the 'Moving School', sitting was alternated with dynamic sitting (53 percent), standing (31 percent) and walking around (10 percent). These children almost never sat bent over at a 45° angle or more. In this school, much more movement was applied during lessons. The conclusion was that sitting behaviours in the second school were more favourable. This group spent much less time sitting in the same position. The children in this group also twisted their backs and necks less frequently, and they were much more mobile (Cardon *et al.*, 2004).

Part III

WHAT ELSE CAN YOU DO? LAYOUT, ORGANIZATION AND DIDACTICS

In Part II you have seen how simple most strategies are which you can use to remedy disrupted sensory processing. But there are many more possibilities for paying attention to sensory processing within the learning environment. In this part, we would like to show you how you can take into account the influence of the senses on attention and focus, and how you can integrate sensory processing in all lessons and coach the students in this, all within your teaching routine. So, really learning with all eight senses. We think this starts when you enter the classroom and it ends with taking a test. Therefore, that is precisely how this part is structured.

8

Layout of the Classroom

 What's this chapter about?

We start this chapter with an exercise in which you will view the class-room through SPI-Glasses. We then explain how the layout influences sensory processing. Again we make a distinction between activating and calming aspects. Involving the students in classroom set-up is discussed and we look at good positions for the under- and overresponsive student. The corridor is also discussed as a possibility. In addition, we pay attention to the place of the teacher in the classroom and to the organization of materials.

  TO DO: THE CLASSROOM

Take a look at the room through SPI-Glasses. The layout of the room has a big effect on the senses. How bright is the light, how hot or cold is it, what view does a student have? To feel the effect of the layout, you can enter the answers to the questions in the following form.

Sit in a student's spot (do this at different spots).

How does the room feel from this place?

_____

_____

_____

_____

Do you feel comfortable and safe? Why is this?

_____

_____

_____

_____

What can and can't you see well from this spot?

_____

_____

_____

_____

Would you like to sit in this spot? Why or why not?

_____

_____

_____

_____

Stand in the doorway to get a good view of the room.

What impression would the room give someone who comes here for the first time?

_____

_____

_____

_____

Would this person like to cross the threshold to look around? Why or why not?

_____

_____

_____

_____

Would this person consider the room activating or calming? Why?

_____

_____

_____

_____

The influence of layout

The layout of a room has a certain effect on people. One layout is more activating while another is more calming. This applies to all spaces, your classroom included. To make you more aware of this, we provide examples of the effect of layout below. We list the things that are respectively more activating and more calming.

The list of activating design aspects shows input which gets the stamp 'very interesting' and 'VIP'. As a result, the underresponsive student becomes more alert and absorbs more information. The overresponsive student is already activated enough and can become hyper-alert in an activating environment.

The list of calming design aspects shows input which is generally considered 'boring'. For the underresponsive student, this layout means they do not receive the extra information they need. For the overresponsive student, this layout is pleasant; it doesn't distract them.

> *In general, it's best to create a quiet environment.*

In this list we show which aspects contribute to an activating or calming layout. Naturally, the classroom will not have a completely activating or calming layout. In reality, it is usually a mix of both. Of course, it is difficult to find exactly the right balance. You will always have a group of students who function better in an environment with little input and a group that benefits from a lot of input and strong input. That is why you must choose between activating and calming aspects. Where do you leave empty space and where do you place extra input? Because the design is ultimately a combination, you also have to be able to add or remove input for the individual student. For example, you give a student a kneaded eraser, a hearing protector or a workplace outside the classroom.

You are generally better off creating a quiet environment, because it is easier to add activating input. For example, it is easier to let students do moving exercises or to add sound than it is to adjust a busy wall or a brightly coloured curtain.

The layout of the room, activating

- Bright sunlight or bright artificial lighting.
- Bright, intense colours and many (fluorescent) colours.
- Curtains with busy prints.
- Open cupboards with multi-coloured content.
- Lots of decorations and crafts on the walls, windows and the ceiling.
- Interactive whiteboard with quickly moving images, a dancing screensaver.
- Many loose things in the room: on the cupboards, on the windowsills, on the floor, on the tables.
- Extra air circulation through open windows and doors or by using a fan.
- Sound from the ventilation system.
- Open doors with a view of people passing by.
- Semi-open doors, so everyone can walk in and out freely.
- Windows onto the corridor, so you can see everything that happens there.
- Hard, smooth floor and other smooth surfaces that reflect sound.
- Low temperature: cool temperatures have an activating

INTERESTING

effect. However, when it is too cold, so much energy goes into warming up the body that there is none left for learning.

The layout of the room, calming

- Soft and/or natural lighting.
- Pastel colours, light colours.
- Plain curtains or curtains with a calm print.
- Plain curtains in front of bookshelves and shelves with toys.
- Closed cabinets.
- Few wall decorations and moving items.
- Crafts are on display in a cabinet.
- The interactive whiteboard is only visible when in use.
- A calming image on the interactive whiteboard, such as a fireplace, sea, cloudy sky or aquarium.
- A tidy room where everything has a clear, assigned place.
- Few things on the tables.
- Closed doors.
- A reversible sign on the door, with 'welcome' on one side and 'do not disturb' on the other, to clarify when walk-ins are really unwanted.
- Foil on the windows to limit views of busy places (the auditorium, a busy junction).
- Background noise muted by:

BORING
USEFUL

- rugs, floor coverings, curtains, acoustic panels and tiles that reduce sound reflection
- hard foam or soft rubber under the computer to reduce the sounds of vibration
- fan/air conditioning off when silence is desired
- fan/air conditioning on for white noise, to mask other disruptive noises
- turning down the volume of the school bell or putting foam over the speaker
- tennis balls or chair glides on the bottom of chair legs to dampen the scraping sound.
- Neutral temperature, not too hot and not too cold. When you are too hot, you get sleepy.

What do the students think of the layout?

Students have their own view on the room in which they spend so much time; they experience it in their own way. Asking for their opinion can provide very interesting information. When the students have been in the classroom for six to eight weeks and have become somewhat used to it, you can ask them how they experience the classroom. But only do this if you can really do something with their ideas. Be realistic and honest with the students; it is probably not possible to act on everything they come up with.

There are different ways to get their opinion. Have the students:

- draw the pleasant and unpleasant things
- explain how they are being distracted
- write a story about what helps them to learn better
- take photos of the room and divide them into 'pleasant' and 'unpleasant'
- identify where they prefer to be seated and explain why.

You don't have to limit this to the classroom; students certainly have an opinion about the rest of the school and probably also ideas about how things can be done there. Following their inventory, you can take it a step further and ask students to:

- make a wishing wall on which they depict how they could feel even more comfortable. Have them think of all the senses and add things about posture, movement, smelling, seeing and hearing

- make a drawing of the desired situation, with captions and an explanation
- make a list/story with tips and tricks about things in the classroom/at school:
  - Where do you hear everyone well?
  - What smells good?
  - Is the temperature pleasant?
  - Are you comfortable sitting at your desk?

All this information can provide surprising insights into possibilities for improving the layout.

Claiming a good spot

We might not think about it often, but students do spend hours and hours of their lives in that particular spot in the classroom. And sitting comfortably isn't the same for everyone. One person is comfortable with their back to the wall and another is more comfortable facing the wall. All the more reason to pay attention to what they choose. Look at the location in the room where the student is sitting. If the student is under- or overresponsive, consult with them when choosing a spot and take the following into account:

For the underresponsive student

- Place this student at a desk:
  - near the door: every time someone walks through the door, they receive extra input
  - near the window: they can find extra input by looking outside, and when the window is open they can feel the wind
  - near walkways
  - with a view of a large part of the room, so they don't have to turn around to look for visual input (to see what is happening in the room)
  - close to you, so you can involve them without too much effort
  - with enough space to wiggle.

- Put a mirror in front of the student; during independent work, this can provide enough extra input to keep working.
- Literally demarcate spaces for a student who cannot properly recognize the personal space of others: use lines on the ground to help them with this.

For the overresponsive student

- Place this student at a desk:
    - with a maximum overview of what is happening in the room, so the student does not have to be afraid of unexpected touch
    - where (almost) nobody has to pass behind them
    - close to a wall, with their back or side facing the wall
    - some distance away from fellow students
    - next to a quiet student; perhaps another overresponsive student, because they often have the same needs
    - at the outside or edge of the group
    - with a view of the door, so they have an overview of what is happening
    - away from air ducts, loud radiators, direct sunlight.
- Take light into account. Is the student bothered by bright sunlight at any time of the day? Are proper sun blinds available?
- Have the student work in a sheltered workplace without a view

of wall decorations and moving items. This is suitable for tasks where they must be able to properly close themselves off from input around them. A sheltered spot can mean the student uses a foldable concentration screen, or sits between partitions or in a corner of the room, for example behind a cupboard.

In many schools, student switch places a few times a year. This can be a stressful event, especially for the overresponsive student. It may take a while before they are used to the new spot. For the underresponsive student, changing places means they are going to experience new input, which is pleasant for them. However, the underresponsive student can learn how to keep themselves active in a spot in the classroom where they receive less input.

Guide the student and discuss how they experience the new spot and which adjustments can help them feel 'at home'.

Leaving them in their familiar spot may seem better, but isn't our preference. Helping students cope is better than avoiding. It is a good thing to not always create separate places or make exceptions, but to use simple adjustments to ensure all students come into their own right in new situations. This way, the students learn what they can do themselves to feel comfortable in different situations. After all, later in life, they will often encounter situations in which it is not possible to find a separate or suitable place. And if they know from experience that they can apply solutions themselves, they will be able to face such new situations in a more relaxed manner.

Sitting ergonomically

Naturally, the ergonomics of sitting also requires attention. Make sure the student has a chair and desk of the correct height. On a regular chair, they must be able to put their feet flat on the floor while their thighs are horizontal. There are also chairs which support an active sitting position – the thighs point diagonally downwards, for a better upright sitting position. In both cases, the elbows must be able to rest on the table without the stu-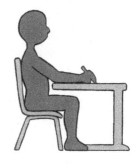
dent having to bend over and without pushing the shoulders up.

Working on a tablet

More and more students work on a tablet in class. It can be difficult to hold the tablet and concentrate on the assignment at the same time. There are various options for supporting the tablet. The student will then have their hands free to operate the tablet. When the student adopts a bad posture while working with a tablet, a tablet support can provide a solution. There are different solutions for working with a tablet support:

- On the desk: a stand, a cover or a flexible bracket that can be attached to the desk.
- Working standing up: a wall bracket or a flexible stand placed on the floor.
- On your lap: a support that rests on your legs. The latter is an ergonomically less desirable solution.

The hallway is not for punishment

In the past, students were put in the hallway for punishment. We also like to send them to the hallway, but not for punishment; the hallway is in fact perfectly suited to movement possibilities or a quiet workplace.

Activating in the hallway

- As an extra movement possibility, have the student do odd jobs which require them to get out of the classroom for a bit, for example getting a book from the library.
- Place a tennis ball on a broomstick: have the student polish the black stripes off the linoleum.
- Have the student walk back and forth in the corridor with giant steps.
- Have the student use a toilet that is further away.

Calming down in the hallway

- If it is a bit too noisy in the classroom, the student can work in the hallway, provided that it is quiet there at that time.
- Have the overresponsive student who shows an emotional reaction calm down in the hallway, for example by letting them walk up and down the stairs until they feel calm again.

- Have them relax in a quiet corner in the hallway, where they can listen to music, for example, or do a puzzle.

> *Put on the SPI-Glasses for yourself and look around the room. Where do you want to sit comfortably?*

And how comfortable are you?

It seems so logical that you, the teacher are in front of the class. But the most important thing is that you sit somewhere where you feel comfortable. Through the tests and theory from Part 1 you now also know approximately what type you are. Put on the SPI-Glasses for yourself and look around the room. Where do you want to sit comfortably?

Please note the following when choosing:

- The location of your desk says nothing about the spot from which you teach. You can sit or stand anywhere to make contact with the students. A roller seat can be useful here.
- Try different spots in the classroom. A certain spot may seem good, initially, but you might sit even better in the other corner.
- Take the seasons into account. A spot that is nice for you in winter can be annoying in summer or vice versa. So, go ahead and completely reorganize the room.
- For you, as well, ask the question: do you have a good seat height? Cushions and footboards can make a world of difference for your back.
- Your desk has various functions, such as helpdesk, discussion spot and quiet place. You can indicate with a flag or a symbol which function your desk has at a certain moment.
- Perhaps you enjoy having a few personal items in the room and you choose to buy them or bring them yourself. It's important to make your classroom somewhere you enjoy spending time.

Organizing materials in the classroom

By now, the tables and chairs are all placed in good spots. But there are still a lot of other things and materials in the room: the rubbish bin, books, workbooks, notebooks, sheets of paper, coloured pencils, erasers, pencils, plants and much more – stuff on tables, in cupboards, drawers and on shelves. Think about this: what effect do all these things have on the students' sensory processing and on your own peace of mind? Below, we provide tips for organizing loose materials for the under- and overresponsive student.

Organizing materials for the underresponsive student

It is difficult for the underresponsive student to keep an overview and to organize their things themselves.

- Have another student help them organize work/drawers/homework. An overresponsive student can help them with this, because they can do this very well.
- Teach the student to put everything away in fixed places.
- Label drawers or put pictures on them, so it is clear what is in them: workbooks, reading book, books, pencil and eraser, etc.
- Use a pencil case or tray for the small items in the drawers.
- Place a pencil case with pencils, a ruler and eraser on the table when there is no space in the drawers, or when they get lost among the other items.
- Take the time to tidy and organize the drawers every week. This will go faster every time (and save time for the rest of the week).
- Use laminated cards as a guide, which have the required materials for different assignments written on them:
  - Maths: 'workbook, notebook, pencil, ruler, eraser, chewing material'
  - Reading: 'reading book, reading ruler, wobble cushion'
  - Worksheet: 'worksheet, coloured pencils, pencil, eraser'.
- Place the notebook or book with which you should work on a contrasting surface (coloured cardboard, for example). The contrast directs the student's attention to their work.

Organizing materials for the overresponsive student

The overresponsive student is very good at organizing their tasks themselves. This gives them a sense of safety and reduces the chance of encountering unknown input.

- Make sure the student has storage materials. Boxes with labels, pencil cases, folders and the like. This way, they can organize everything in a structured manner.

- Have the student only put those materials on their desk which they are currently working with.
- Make sure that tools are within reach (chewing chain, hearing protection, fidget material).
- Provide spare materials, so the student doesn't panic if something runs out or breaks.
- To provide structure, use laminated cards that state what is needed for different assignments:
  - Maths: 'workbook, notebook, pencil, ruler, eraser, chewing material'
  - Reading: 'reading book, reading ruler, concentration screen'
  - Worksheet: 'worksheet, coloured pencils, pencil, eraser, work standing at the cupboard'.

To organize the loose items in the room, you can use crates and boxes on which you write the contents with a marker. You can buy hanging shoe organizers in which you can store a lot of small things. Some shoe boxes have a small window in the front, so you can see what's inside. And a magazine rack is also a great place for storing papers.

To organize all the papers and things on your own desk, you can use coloured folders, boxes and crates. For example, yellow is for student affairs, green is for class administration and purple is for school subjects. This makes it a clear system for everyone.

9

Organize the Classroom

What's this chapter about?

In this chapter, we provide tips to organize your class in a way which improves sensory processing. We start this chapter with the desk arrangement. We explain why it is worthwhile to spend time on this. We give tips on how you can help the under- and overresponsive student better organize their work. We explain how you can provide instructions in an activating and calming way and show how you can use fixed rituals to get and hold the attention of the students. We also provide tips on how to keep your students involved when they have to listen for a long time.

The (desk) arrangement matters

All kinds of clever minds reflect on the different work methods during class. For example, you start with a learning conversation and then switch to group work. This then requires a different layout of the room. Unfortunately, this does not always happen. Because, let's be honest, do you change the arrangement of the furniture along with the work method?

LITERATURE ABOUT REORGANIZING THE CLASSROOM

Teachers estimate the duration of changing the set-up is twice as long as it actually is. Experience from many teachers shows that an entire classroom can be converted without too much noise within one to two minutes (Ebbens and Ettekoven, 2013).

We regularly see classrooms where students sit with their backs to the teacher and the interactive whiteboard. Or students who have to do group work sitting in a row. If this is the case, the work method is much less successful. In fact, it causes confusion. This happens because the desk arrangement sends a mixed message. For example, if students are sitting with their backs to the board, the message is:

- I am now going to explain something that is so complicated that I have to use the whiteboard.
- It is not that important for you to follow my explanation, because I think it's alright if some students cannot see this.

Quite difficult for the student to understand... Fortunately, the reverse is also true: the following message is very positive:

- I am now going to explain something that is so complicated that I have to use the whiteboard.
- It is so important that everyone can follow my explanation that I want to reorganize the entire room to achieve this.

> *Moving furniture offers a great opportunity to move around.*

It is extra strenuous for sensory processing when the body's posture doesn't match the work method. It is complicated to be looking over your shoulder or having to bend or turn your head to get information. This makes it more difficult for the brain to pay attention to the lesson. It is already working hard to keep the body balanced or to catch words clearly.

So, it really is very important for the arrangement of the tables and chairs and the work method to match. Below, you can see illustrations of possible set-ups.

Our strategy is: make a virtue of necessity! Moving furniture offers a great opportunity to move around. It also fluently indicates the transition from, for example, working with the whole class to independent working time. And it offers time for the memory to process the learned material.

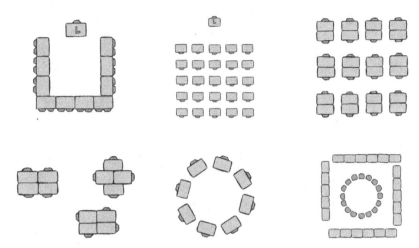

From Ebbens and Ettekoven, 2013

How can you drag and push practically?

- Have the students make a number of floor plans according to your instruction, so you can indicate the desired layout of the desks and chairs.

- Coloured stickers on the wall or on the floor, which align with the various arrangements, help get the desks in the right place.
- Put the underresponsive student to work and have them drag and push furniture.

- The overresponsive student may quietly stand aside or leave the classroom for a while. Or give them a task which doesn't require them to be in the middle of the action, such as getting the books and notebooks for the next lesson.
- Practise moving everything around several times at the beginning of the school year and time the process. Timing this is a great task for an overresponsive student. How long does it take until everyone is sitting in the right place (quietly and not moving)?
- Moving the furniture is easy to do in three steps:
  a. Put loose items from the desk in the drawer.
  b. Bring the desk to the new spot in the room.
  c. Bring the chair to the new spot in the room.
- You can also give students certain tasks: one group handles the desks; another handles the chairs. Or one group does the right front of the room and another group does the right back, and so on.

Quartets, trios and uh...a twosome?

So, you had it all figured out: from now on, drawing will be done in groups of four. It looked so beautiful in your head. However, you hadn't taken into consideration the number of desks, so it just didn't work out. It might go the same way with other work methods and rearrangement plans. So, by all means, use trial and error working together with the students. A few focus points:

- Groups of desks must be placed with enough space left over to walk between them.
- For you as a teacher it is useful to use an office chair or roller seat. You can easily move around on these, so that you can quickly move to a student and help them out.
- It is nice to keep a small area free around the whole set-up, so you can walk or stand there to have an overview.
- Desks aren't necessary for everything. Students can also write or draw for a little while on their lap, on a flat surface (a book).
- The teacher's desk can also be in the centre or at the back of the room.

A reorganized room, a new start

Perhaps this class has had a bit of a rough time and shuffling everything around helps clean the slate for a fresh start. From a social point of view, shuffling things around can be instrumental to help influence group dynamics. If students know they will not be sitting next to their friend forever, it might cause other social behaviour. This requires a little more adjustment from the overresponsive student than from the underresponsive student. But practice makes perfect and the student learns how to deal with change with your support.

A matter of organizing

Throughout the entire day, switching between activities and therefore switching materials takes place. First, only a notebook is needed, then the desk needs to be empty, and next, a textbook, workbook and pencil are required. This means the student must organize their materials while doing their work. This area also leaves room for tips for both the under- and overresponsive student.

For the underresponsive student

- Write down instructions or use pictures or icons, so the student can always look back to check what the assignment was.

- Divide the assignment into smaller tasks to help the student keep an overview.
- After a certain number of assignments, ask the student to show their work. This can be to the teacher, but also to a classmate.

This gives an opportunity to move and talk and ensures that the student stays the right kind of busy.

- Have the student draw as many boxes on a piece of paper as there are assignments. After each assignment they can colour in a box. Or they can string paperclips together, adding a new one for every assignment, or move coins from one container to another. They will have as many paperclips/coins as assignments.
- Use laminated cards they can refer to when they no longer know what to do. For example, they might say:
  a. Do I know what to do? (Otherwise, I will ask.)
  b. What do I need? (Pencil, eraser, notebook, chewing material.)
  c. Clean up the desk.
  d. Do five push-ups in my seat.
  e. Start the assignment.
  f. Do two push-ups in my chair every five minutes.
- Use different lists for fixed routines to ensure they get used to the routine, so at some point the list can be thrown out (after a little goodbye party, of course).
- Have the student make a habit of checking with others whether everything is correct: whether they are doing the right task, have written down the right information, have grabbed everything they need.
- Have the student think about solutions to properly organize their materials. Initiative and involvement are motivating and increase alertness.

For the overresponsive student

- Have them work alone.
- Use a timer for difficult tasks. The student is better able to persist in their task when they know how long they will have to go on for.
- Split the assignment up into smaller tasks to help the student keep an overview.
- Have the student cross off tasks on a list. This suits the overresponsive student's need for structure. Do not use paper

clips or coins here; they provide more input and the desk can soon become too cluttered.

- Write down instructions or use pictures or icons to give a good overview.
- Use laminated cards that the student can refer to. For example, they might say:
  a. Do I know what to do?
  b. What do I need for the assignment? (Pencil, eraser, notebook, hearing protector.)
  c. Clean up the desk.
  d. Lay out the hearing protector.
  e. Start the assignment.
  f. If I need it, put on a hearing protector.
  g. When I'm done, I can read or do a puzzle.
- Make sure the student can anticipate what is coming.
- Tell the student in advance if a fire drill with a loud alarm is coming up and lay out a hearing protector.
- Explain in advance how an unknown activity will happen: when will it be over? What are we going to do next (something familiar)?

'Guys, wake up!'

When receiving instructions, it is very important that the student is focused. Their attention shouldn't dwindle. Because if you miss part of the instructions, you won't know what to do later in the lesson. The teacher can help by giving instructions in a sensory-friendly manner.

Below, we provide tips for adjusting the instructions to activate students. You do this when the student needs some extra sensory input, for example because they watched an introductory film, during which they had to passively sit still. The tips can be applied both for the whole class and individually.

You give instructions in an activating manner by:

- making quick movements
- using sharp contrasts in materials or on the (interactive) whiteboard. Use instruction materials and (interactive) whiteboard images in black and white or with bright colours, instead of greys and soft colours

- varying volume, tone and rhythm of voice or audio
- introducing unpredictable, unexpected and new things, for example suddenly giving instructions while singing
- using light touch
- letting touch come as a surprise (of course, not with the overresponsive student, but you probably don't have to activate them as often).

'Guys, calm down please!'

Below, we provide tips for adjusting the instructions to calm down students. There are times when peace and quiet are required in the classroom, for example when something funny took place outside and caused a commotion. Everyone will have to calm down before you can start teaching again. The tips can be applied both for the whole class and individually.

You give instructions in a calming manner by:

- using repetition
- allowing moments of silence
- moving slowly
- using a soft, monotonous voice with consistent volume
- speaking at a slow pace, in a low tone
- being predictable (performing actions in a fixed order ensures the student knows what is going to happen)
- indicating how long an activity will take
- taking more time for certain activities
- talking for a shorter period
- not letting touch come as a surprise: approach the student slowly and in their field of vision
- using firm touch
- being at the student's eye level.

Fixed rituals in class

Teachers often have small rituals to get their students' undivided attention. These small rituals are used at many different times:

- as an announcement for fixed times of the day ('We will clean up in five minutes')
- to explain something during a task ('You can skip question 6, we'll do that later')
- to restore order ('It is getting a bit rowdy, everyone quiet again, please!').

An addition to the last point: a tool to use to restore order is a 'noise meter'. You can easily make this yourself by drawing a graph or a coloured rectangle and hang it on the whiteboard or wall, with a line that rises to a 'noise limit'. When that limit is reached, you can remind the students to be quiet. So, you draw this yourself and make the line longer when the noise increases.

A good ritual can help restore disrupted sensory processing. A good ritual offers a moment to 'reset'. The underresponsive student receives a new impulse and knows that certain input is coming. The overresponsive student knows from the ritual that something familiar will follow.

> *A good ritual offers a moment to 'reset'.*

A good ritual must meet a few requirements:

- It must be striking; the ritual must cause a special reaction. If you use 'clapping your hands' to request all the following actions:
  - silence
  - work
  - attention
  - listening
  - speaking

  it is unclear to the students what they should do.
- It must be repeatable. Using a sound on your smartphone is inconvenient if you regularly forget your phone.
- It must be in harmony with the response. So, shouting loudly when asking for silence gives a contradictory message.

There are many opportunities to get students focused on the lesson, which you can apply at different moments:

- Turn the lights off and on again, to signal that everyone must return to their desks.

- Showing a cartoon on the whiteboard that asks for silence.
- Gently clapping your hands to make everyone look to the front.
- Counting backwards together, in a whisper, from ten to one. Gradually all students will start counting with you.
- Tapping the whiteboard to make everyone look at the whiteboard.
- Waving your arms to draw attention to yourself.
- Clapping your hands to signal that discussion time is over.
- Raise your hand when you want attention. Any student who sees this must then also raise their hand (and is no longer allowed to talk). When you lower your hand, the students will do the same.

- A bell or a special sound, possibly installed on your smartphone.
- Holding up a piece of cardboard with text on it (this could also be a task for a student).
- Gently shaking maracas.
- Standing at a certain fixed location in the room.
- Opening or closing the door very emphatically and mentioning it while you're doing it. For example, you close the door at the beginning of the lesson and say, 'Well, the door is closing, we're going to get started now.'

Listening for a looooong time

Sometimes it can be difficult to keep all your students involved in circle time, an evaluation or an educational conversation. Students are easily distracted when they have not had a turn to speak for a while and have only had to passively listen to and watch others. Activating strategies help you in these situations. Are you noticing an increase in unrest or boredom in the group? If so, apply one of the tips below.

Keeping students interested when they have to listen for a long time

- Have the students move around a lot; take every opportunity to do this. Are you singing a song? Sing standing up and make movements that go with the song.
- Have the students stand up occasionally, for example when they are telling a story or giving an answer.
- Are the students sitting in chairs? Halfway through the activity, turn the seats around and have everyone sit on them astride.
- Sit down on the floor for a change. Give everyone their own piece of carpet to sit on and to define their own space.
- Are you sitting on the floor? Then also try:
  - lying on your stomach, resting on your elbows
  - sitting on your knees
  - sitting with your arms around your knees.
- In-between, have everyone stamp their feet (this can be done while sitting or standing).
- Stand up for a moment and have everyone make themselves as tall as possible or shake their bodies.
- Have everyone repeat the answer out loud.
- Is one student finished telling their story? Have all other students applaud; this will wake them up again as well. This could also be an applause using only the fingertips.
- For the fidgeters, tie a shoelace to their chair, so they always have something on hand.
- Have the student stand behind their chair as they listen to you. Direct them to hold the shoelace tied to their chair. This way, you can be certain they will stay in their spot.

- Don't forget the overresponsive student. This student mainly needs space and shouldn't sit next to a restless student. The outside of the semicircle is a good spot, or next to the teacher or a quieter student.

10

Tips for Teaching Methods

What's this chapter about?

In this chapter, we provide didactic tips, so you can make lessons sensory-friendly in an easy way. We start this chapter with a discussion about focus and show how you can take sensory input into account for different work methods. We give suggestions to keep the focus optimized and tell you how you can utilize all the senses in your lessons and assignments. We talk about goal-oriented learning and tests and exams. In conclusion, you will read about the use of humour in the classroom.

TO DO: SIT STILL AND PAY ATTENTION!

It may not stand out that much, but a student actually spends a large part of their day sitting still in their chair. Consider, therefore, how long a student is sitting still during a full lesson. Write down the number of minutes:

- Looking back/retrieving prior knowledge -> _____ minutes

- Overview lesson goals -> _____ minutes

- Introducing new material -> _____ minutes

- Supervised practising -> _____ minutes

- Individual processing of information -> _____ minutes

- Joint review -> _____ minutes

- Discussing the process -> _____ minutes

Total -> _____ minutes

How many minutes does that make? Quite a lot, we think!

You really are busy as a bee!

The result of the exercise may come as a surprise, because you as a teacher actually move around a lot.

- You walk back and forth in front of the digital whiteboard.
- You write, you swipe.
- You point to a student who may answer your question.
- You walk to a desk.
- You squat down.
- You pull up a chair.
- You open a window.
- You pick up a pen from the floor.
- And so forth.

This means that, as a teacher, you have many opportunities for self-regulation through movement. If your focus drops, you can easily go and do something. Therefore, you might not notice that the student spends a lot of time sitting still at their desk during the day. All this time, they are expected to be quite focused, but they have far fewer opportunities to use movement to become more alert.

> *You, the teacher, are actually moving around quite a lot.*

The 10-15-20 minute limit?

The above exercise gives you an idea of how long we expect a student to be able to concentrate during an entire lesson. But is this expectation realistic? Children's concentration span is often overestimated. Researchers do not entirely agree on how long children and adults are able to focus on one task; however, it is shorter than most people think.

Nevertheless, scientists do agree that people can concentrate longer as they age and as they find their tasks more interesting. They can also concentrate longer when they renew their focus on a task after a short distraction. This is how it works: during a distraction you kind of zoom out, like you can do with a camera. The lens refocuses on the complete picture, your brain 'relaxes' and allows other input to enter. You allow your brain a break, after which you can focus on the subject again. Having a small break after 15 minutes and then continuing your task will result in higher learning efficiency than going on for half an hour at once.

Use activating and calming strategies from Chapter 5, 'In the classroom' during these interruptions.

SCIENCE AND CONCENTRATION SPAN

Dukette and Cornish (2009) found that the average time someone can concentrate without getting distracted varies from three to five minutes for young children and up to 20 minutes for adults. This applies to tasks that are interesting and motivating to that person. They also write that adults can concentrate much longer, for example on a two-hour film, because they have 'reset' their concentration through a short distraction.

In a literature review, the widespread assumption that children can concentrate in class for ten to 15 minutes at a time is disproved. The review shows that the studies on which this assumption is based were often not or only indirectly related to concentration span. Also, many cited sources could be traced back to personal observations instead of scientific studies (Wilson and Korn, 2007).

In another study, a decrease in concentration was observed during a lecture after 30 seconds, after four-and-a-half to five-and-a-half minutes, after seven to nine minutes and after nine to ten minutes. Most of the decreases in concentration lasted about one minute and became more frequent the longer the lecture lasted. At the end of the lecture, the short decreases in concentration occurred approximately every two minutes. This study showed that the decrease in concentration was much less at times (and immediately after) when active learning strategies were used, such as during and after demonstrations and asking questions (Bunce, Flens and Neiles, 2010).

Matters of the heart

A student can only learn fully if, for example, they are not chock-full of food, do not urgently need to visit the toilet or feel cold. Although the ability to learn and engage in social behaviour is to some extent related to being able to properly interpret interoceptive stimuli, relatively little attention is paid to this in children's education. You can teach your students a valuable lesson by talking about this topic. Ask what physical sensations they feel when they are tired, or in love, or hungry. Becoming familiar with the signals of interoception, being able to recognize them and act accordingly, will certainly promote learning efficiency and the social climate in the classroom!

Tell your students how strong their organs are. Your heart is able to beat very fast; that's okay, it's not something to be afraid of. You can tell them about walking and running, and how your heart can handle both really well. Also, a full bladder may give you a very uncomfortable feeling in your belly, but although you bladder can 'feel like bursting', it very likely will not burst any time soon if you don't go to the toilet quickly enough. And if you're healthy, you really won't pass out any time soon with hunger. This information may reassure students and help them identify their interoceptive signals.

Learning with your legs

It has been scientifically proven that exercising during a learning activity has a beneficial effect on learning. We explained this in Chapter 7, under 'Strategies and science'. Sitting still and listening for a long time – which students have to do a lot of in class – is therefore not very good for the learning process. It is better to embed a strategy into different moments in your lesson so that students will be activated again. And it's even better to move while learning. When moving, chemicals are released which activate the brain, so more sensory input is passed along in the brain. This allows you to better absorb information and learn. Below are some suggestions.

> *Sitting still and listening for a long time isn't very good for the learning process.*

1. Reviewing/retrieving prior knowledge

- 'Everyone stand with your back to the digital whiteboard for a moment, so we can momentarily "look into the past". What did we learn last time, about...?'
- 'To retrieve the information you learned last time, walk your fingers from your neck over the crown of your head to your forehead. First with your left hand, then with the right and finally with both your hands at the same time.'
- 'We are going to look back, to "see" what we already know about this topic. Bend over and look back through the gap between

your legs. Move back up again. Now we will take a good look once more.'
- 'Stand in pairs:
  - Use keywords to tell each other what you already know about...
  - With your finger, write keywords on each other's back which you remember from the lesson about...
  - Act out what you know about... The person acting out is not allowed to talk.'

2. Overview of the learning goals that are on the board

- 'Let's all stretch towards the learning goals.'
- 'Turn to your neighbour and tell them the learning objective: "At the end of the lesson I can..." Take turns and repeat twice.'
- 'Let's all repeat the learning objectives out loud, all at once!' You can do this in the following ways:
  - happy
  - angry
  - sad
  - surprised
  - whispering
  - rapping
  - ...?

3. Introduce new material with suitable exercises

- 'When we start reading, we are going to wake up our eyes by tapping the lids very gently with our fingertips or by rubbing them.'
- 'When we start maths, we'll wake our fingers by tapping each finger with our other hand.'
- 'For world orientation, today we will be talking about rivers. Let's all make swimming movements with our arms or pretend we're jumping into the water.'

4. Supervised practising

- 'Applaud the student who gave the correct answer.'

- 'Give yourself a hug because you knew the right answer.'
- 'Give yourself a pat on the shoulder because you engaged in the thinking process.'
- 'Shake your neighbour's hand (congratulate them) if they know the right answer.'
- 'The student who will be giving the answer sits down and the rest of the students stand up.'

5. Independent or group work

- 'Use a strategy of your choice to stay alert. For example, you can stand up and continue reading, or do chair push-ups. Everything should be done in silence and only when you feel you need it.'
- 'I'm just going to do some finger gymnastics and stretch.'

6. Joint review

- 'At the start of the review, we will all look through "binoculars". Make two circles with your hands and put them in front of your eyes. Take a good look around the room.'
- 'We're going to look back while standing up.'
- 'Turn your chair around, the back now facing forward, and sit astride it.'

7. Discussing the process

- 'Before we look at how the lesson went, we will walk around the room.'
- 'Circle around on the spot, first to the left and then to the right.'
- 'We're going to touch all parts of ourselves that contributed to this lesson, such as feet, knees, buttocks, abdomen, chest, arms, hands, mouth, ears, nose, eyes and head.'

Proximity and distance senses

We can divide the eight senses into proximity and distance senses. This may sound strange, because after all they are all located in our body. The difference lies in the way the input enters. With distance senses, the input comes from *outside* your body. The distance senses are hearing, sight and smell. Input from light, sounds or smells comes from outside and hits your body through light waves, sound waves or tiny molecules floating in the air.

With proximity senses, the input comes from *within* or *on* your body. The proximity senses are touch, balance, movement, taste and interoception. Your skin gets touched, movement comes from your body and food enters through your mouth.

> *By using proximity senses as well, you provide stronger input.*
> *This way you have a better chance the message will arrive.*

You can use this knowledge on proximity and distance senses to communicate with your student in the classroom and influence their alertness. Because when we want to transfer information, we usually do so by talking and showing things – through the distance senses. This information is not always properly received by the underresponsive student. The input disappears again as soon as the image is gone, or the spoken instruction is over. This makes the information fleeting and difficult to retrieve when the images, smells and sounds are no longer there.

By using proximity senses in communication, you provide stronger input, so you have a better chance the message will arrive. When you're giving one-on-one instructions, you can start with your hand resting calmly but firmly on the student's arm or shoulder. This way, you're giving activating input and you increase the chance that the student focuses their attention all on you. You can also activate the student by having them move a little before you give instructions. This stimulates proximity senses such as balance and movement. This increases alertness, which means information can be registered and processed more effectively.

Learning with your nose

In general, the focus during a lesson is on watching, listening and writing. Therefore, learning with the eyes, ears and fingers. This is quite one-sided. With most forms of instruction, you mainly appeal to the distance senses (hearing and sight). This input isn't strong enough to be considered VIP or very interesting. The input disappears as soon as the image is gone, or the spoken instruction is over. This makes the information fleeting and difficult to retrieve when the images and sounds are no longer there. If, on the other hand, during the instruction you provide information through proximity senses such as touch, balance and movement, the instruction is better registered. This sensory input has an activating effect which persists after the input has ended.

> **Take a critical look at the extent to which your lessons appeal to all eight senses.**

Therefore, take a critical look at the lessons, and assess to what extent they appeal to all eight different senses. How can you adjust this? Here are some examples:

- You can use *touch* during language lessons, by feeling and grasping letters. When the students are still learning the letters, you could have them sculpt all the letters out of clay, or cut them out of paper or fabric. The same applies to numbers during maths.
- During maths lessons you can use *movement* by:
  - counting steps
  - reciting the multiplication tables while marching on the spot
  - seeing how wide the room is in literal feet
  - having the students form a triangle or circle.
- During geography lessons you can use *taste* and *smell* by tasting food from different countries. During history lessons you can taste and smell food from the past. In biology lessons you can use, for instance, mushrooms and edible flowers.
- During history lessons you can use *balance* by posing as living statues, depicting historical figures. During maths, multiplication tables can be recited while standing on one leg.
- During nature lessons you can use *smell* by having students smell different flowers, plants or sea water. During history lessons you can smell a scent from the past, for example charcoal.
- During biology lessons you can have children eat fruit during a lesson on the digestive system and have them feel the difference before and after eating. Or drink three glasses of water and see who will be the last to use the toilet.

Solutions can also be found for lessons where appealing to a different sense is less obvious. For example, let students eat a raisin during such lessons, or have them smell their own knees.

Feeling your project

It is a fun challenge for students to involve their senses in all kinds of assignments. A fixed part of the assignment can be, for example, to have the student or audience use at least three senses. Ears and eyes will almost always be a part of this, but now the other senses will also be used alternately. In this way, students become aware of the different sensory inputs that exist and how they can cause those themselves. This can be done during many different assignments:

- Paper/presentation: offer something to smell, taste, feel, have everyone move along.
- Project: add something that can be touched, describe how something smells or tastes.
- Visual artwork/craft project: touch different materials, carry them around, create something that moves and imitate it with your own body.
- Film: move along with the main character, have people smell scents that occur in the film.
- Music/drama: use smell or taste in the theatre too; tap your feet to the beat.

Yay, a learning goal!

Learning is fun. Soon, you can do something, or you know something that you couldn't do or didn't know before. If students are aware of this, they enjoy having such a goal. A learning goal provides students with a positive challenge (Hattie, 2013). It must be a clear learning objective though, and this isn't always the case: sometimes lesson goals and learning goals are confused.

A *lesson goal* is usually a means to achieve a learning goal. For example, students concentrate on completing task 4, drawing your mouth (lesson goal), which helps them learn how their own digestive system works (learning goal). Therefore, always start off telling students why they are going to read a story, watch a video or go on an excursion. What will they eventually learn? And how does this activity help? To clarify the *learning goal*, you can discuss the answers to these questions in advance:

- What are you going to learn? You can make this question clearer (and more interesting) by being very explicit:
  - What will you know or understand soon?
  - What can you do from now on?
  - What ideas will you have on the topic?
- Why are you learning this?
- With whom will you learn this?
- When will you learn this?
- How are you going to learn this? You can ask the under- and overresponsive student for tips: Which strategies can you use to achieve this learning goal?

This way, students learn to be more involved in their learning process and to enjoy it more. They experience a feeling of success when they have achieved the learning goal. The under- or overresponsive student in particular can learn, assisted by you, how to use suitable strategies.

Assessments and tests

Being assessed or tested is an exciting event for many students. Of course, this also applies to the under- or overresponsive student. Together, try to think in advance about which strategies could help them to cope and come to an agreement about this. For suitable strategies, see Chapter 5, 'In your chair'.

Before the test, you can help the students. Prepare a range of tools so students know there is plenty to fiddle and wiggle with. A student can then place items of choice on their desk. Place extra items in a special spot in the classroom, such as hearing protection and sunglasses. The student can then point something out if they need a tool.

If the student knows supportive tools are available, it is reassuring to them. Sometimes so much so, that they don't even need them. Knowing that the possibility is there is enough.

It also feels good to approach the assessment or test as a team, consisting of teacher and student. As a teacher, you signal that you're doing everything you can to ensure that the student performs as well as possible. This can make the student feel supported. You could even turn it into a game, including a plan of attack and tactical discussions. Discuss with the student: 'How are we going to approach this? What plan can we make for this?'

Guidelines provide direction

Help the student who needs more support to be able to (continue to) work independently by visualizing the assignment. Put icons or pictures with information on the wall or on the board so students can see them or put them on their own table. Create icons or images for:

- noise level (silent, whispering or talking normally)
- working independently/working in pairs/group work
- personal planning or book/notebook planned by the teacher
- page numbers (written with a whiteboard marker)
- assignment numbers
- clock (fill in what time the activity will finish)
- whom or how you can ask for help (raise your hand/consult with classmate)
- how it will be marked (teacher checks/check it yourself/ classmate checks/check with the whole class)
- what you can do if you finish early.

This makes working easier for both the under- and overresponsive student; both benefit from clarity.

Humour in the classroom

> *When you use humour, students remember information better and longer.*

Laughter is healthy for the body. But this isn't all there is to it: by using humour, students also remember information better and longer (Jonas, 2009). Laughter is therefore truly an important tool for learning. Laughing can help the overresponsive student discharge and calm down. It activates the underresponsive student. By using humour, you can greatly increase the acceptance of each other's sensory preferences. You do this by joking about your own 'oddities' and involving the students in this. By drawing attention to your own under- or overresponsivity, you can encourage students to get to know their own preferences for sensory input. For example, have the class count the number of times you have lost your glasses or pen in one day. By using humour consciously, students can get to know each other's being different in a respectful way and it becomes open for discussion.

A few tips for using humour:

- Find funny pictures or anecdotes before the lesson, for example about the senses.
- Exaggerate your sensory preferences until it becomes quite ridiculous.
- Ask students to depict a sense in a funny way.
- Ask students to depict an under- or overresponsive celebrity or historical figure in a funny way. First, try to guess what their preference will be: do you think Donald Duck needs more or less input?
- Do a laughing exercise: have the students laugh out loud. Everyone will be laughing for real in no time. Make sure you stay in control and that the laughter decreases after a while.
- Make a joke jar: print jokes about the senses or write them on a piece of paper, fold them in half and put them in a jar. As a reward, students can take a piece of paper from the jar and read it to the class.
- Have 'joke minutes': have students tell jokes for a few minutes. Of course, preferably jokes that incorporate the senses in some way.
- Recall funny moments: 'Do you remember when…?'

Part IV

THE TEACHER WITH SPI-GLASSES

In this last part of the book, we connect the theory with everyday practice. We want you to be able to put on the SPI-Glasses – which you are now very familiar with – in everyday situations at school. Cooperation with parents is discussed; the SPI-Glasses also come in handy here. Sometimes you and the parent each see the child very differently and that may have everything to do with (your) sensory processing

11

Practice Makes Perfect

What's this chapter about?

In this chapter, we practise using the SPI-viewing guide (see Chapter 4) and choosing strategies in specific situations. We do this based on six case studies, which take place inside and outside the classroom. First, we practise characterizing the student: do they need a strategy? If so, is this an *activating* or *calming* strategy? Then you choose which strategies you could use in the situations described for each student.

Characterizing the student

Here, we repeat the SPI-viewing guide from Chapter 4 so it's easier for you to consult it.

The SPI-viewing guide

The child is displaying disruptive behaviour

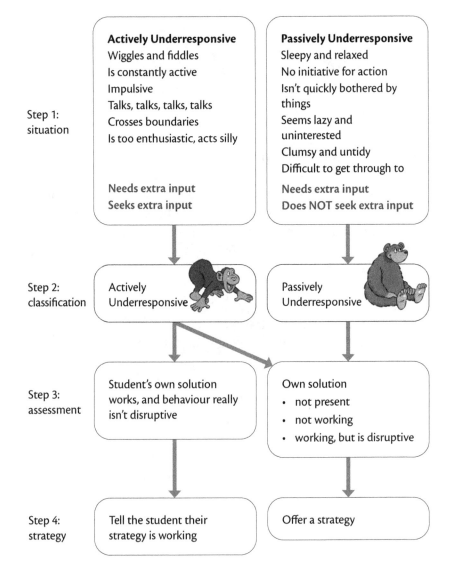

Step 1: situation

Actively Underresponsive
Wiggles and fiddles
Is constantly active
Impulsive
Talks, talks, talks, talks
Crosses boundaries
Is too enthusiastic, acts silly

Needs extra input
Seeks extra input

Passively Underresponsive
Sleepy and relaxed
No initiative for action
Isn't quickly bothered by things
Seems lazy and uninterested
Clumsy and untidy
Difficult to get through to

Needs extra input
Does NOT seek extra input

Step 2: classification

Actively Underresponsive

Passively Underresponsive

Step 3: assessment

Student's own solution works, and behaviour really isn't disruptive

Own solution
• not present
• not working
• working, but is disruptive

Step 4: strategy

Tell the student their strategy is working

Offer a strategy

The child is displaying disruptive behaviour

Step 1: situation

Actively Overresponsive
Not flexible, wants routine
Makes decisions easily
Notices every (little) change
Is easily annoyed
Refuses, often doesn't want to come (or play) along
Wants to determine how things go

Is bothered by input
Avoids input

Passively Overresponsive
Responds to everything in their environment
Easily angered, grumbles, cries
Impressions last for a long time
Likes to be on their own
Things often 'suddenly' become too much
Becomes fearful easily

Is bothered by input
Does NOT avoid input

Step 2: classification

Actively Overresponsive

Passively Overresponsive

Step 3: assessment

Student's own solution works, and behaviour really isn't disruptive

Own solution
• not present
• not working
• works, but is disruptive

Step 4: strategy

Tell the student their strategy is working

Offer a strategy

TO DO: CLASSIFYING THE STUDENT THROUGH THE SPI-VIEWING GUIDE

First of all, we will practise classifying the student. How can the student's behaviour tell you what is going on with them? We have written out six situations for you below. First, read about the situation and see which behaviour takes place. Then, look at the SPI-viewing guide and ask yourself the following questions:

1. Is the student underresponsive or overresponsive?
2. Why did you come to the classification of being under- or overresponsive?
3. Does the student show self-regulation?
4. Does this self-regulation work sufficiently?
5. Is the self-regulation disruptive?
6. What is needed now? No strategy (but feedback to the student that what they are doing is working well for them), or an activating or calming strategy?

Now look at which classification suits the student and explain why. Of course, you can also do this exercise with colleagues and compare results.

Our answers can be found at the end of the chapter. We will classify the student and their needs. We will add an explanation every time.

1. Saadia: Working together in groups
Situation
The students are working in the classroom, creating a maths game. The students are discussing the division of tasks; the teacher is walking around. The students are working in groups of four; Saadia is working with three other students.

Behaviour
Saadia:

- tells the others what to do
- gives herself the task of looking things up
- makes sure others will do the gluing and painting
- isn't very open to negotiation
- has very clear and well-defined ideas
- has a good overview of what needs to be done
- asks other groups to be more quiet.

Classification

_____

_____

Explanation

_____

_____

_____

_____

2. Bart: Working independently in the classroom
Situation

All students are working independently in the classroom. Some text must be read, and questions must be answered. It is quiet in the room. The teacher has checked whether everyone understands the assignment. Most students have already written something in their notebook, but Bart has not written down anything at all yet.

Behaviour
Bart:

- looks in his book, stares out the window, looks around the room
- bites his pencil
- looks at his book again, seems to be reading
- fiddles with the zipper of his hoody
- shifts in his seat
- gets up and starts sharpening his pencil
- asks if he can go to the toilet.

Classification

_____

_____

Explanation

_____

_____

_____

_____

3. Lynn: Instructions to the entire class
Situation
In the classroom, the teacher is giving instructions, which requires everyone to listen and look at the digital whiteboard. The teacher points at things on the board and provides examples. The students have a book and notebook in front of them, which they occasionally look at. The teacher is the only one who talks and moves.

Behaviour
Lynn:

- sits at her table and looks sleepily from the whiteboard to her book
- draws something in her notebook
- accidentally pushes her book off the desk
- sees her pencil also roll off the desk
- briefly engages with the teacher, when the teacher attempts to make contact, but is almost immediately distracted again.

Classification

_____

_____

Explanation

_____

_____

_____

_____

4. Lidy: Going home
Situation
It is the end of the day and everyone is in the corridor. All students must put on their coats, pack their things and walk down the stairs to the door leading outside. They will be picked up outside. Lidy is standing at the door of the classroom.

Behaviour
Lidy:

- delays when she leaves the classroom, because she does not want to get stuck in the bustle
- doesn't want to wait when she's stuck in the bustle, she wants to go down the corridor quickly
- takes her coat, but forgets the other things she must take with her
- is quick to start a row
- grumbles
- does not want to shake the teacher's hand
- does not talk to the teacher at the door.

Classification

_____

_____

Explanation

_____

_____

_____

_____

5. Jamal: Playing football in the playground
Situation
Jamal participates in a game of football in the playground. He plays very roughly. He pushes a fellow student, who then falls and has a bleeding knee. A fight starts. The fellow student cries; he and Jamal must report to the teacher.

Behaviour

Jamal:

- has no idea that he is too rough in his play
- *always* plays roughly, according to the fellow student
- regularly comes too close to others; he has no idea of personal space
- is sad, but above all indignant and really thinks he did nothing wrong.

Classification

_____

_____

Explanation

_____

_____

_____

_____

6. Arthur: In the dressing room

Situation

Arthur is in the dressing room with his classmates, where they are getting changed for PE.

Behaviour

Arthur:

- chooses a place in the empty half of the dressing room, where the next class will soon be changing clothes
- does not respond to comments from his classmates
- changes clothes in silence
- is done quickly and then walks towards the almost empty PE hall
- sits down on a bench at the side.

Classification

_____

_____

Explanation

_____

_____

_____

_____

TO DO: CHOOSE STRATEGIES

Now that you have determined the classification, you can practise offering the right strategy. We have once more written down the situations below, but now with the classification included. Read through this information again and write in each box which strategies you think are suitable. Consider which strategies you could use in advance and which during the activity. For strategies in the classroom, check Chapter 5. You can consult Chapter 6 for strategies outside the classroom. Our answers can be found at the end of this section. There are several correct answers, as long as they match the classification. You choose activating strategies for the underresponsive student and calming strategies for the overresponsive student.

1. Saadia: Working together in groups
Situation
The students are working in the classroom, creating a maths game. The students are discussing the division of tasks; the teacher is walking around. The students are working in groups of four; Saadia is working with three other students.

Classification
Saadia is overresponsive and active. Her self-regulation is not entirely sufficient; Saadia could use some extra calming strategies.

Strategies in advance

_____

_____

_____

_____

Strategies during

_____

_____

_____

_____

2. Bart: Working independently in the classroom
Situation
All students are working independently in the classroom. Some text must be read, and questions must be answered. It is quiet in the room. The teacher has checked whether everyone understands the assignment. Most students have already written something in their notebook, but Bart has not written down anything at all yet.

Classification
Bart is underresponsive and active. His self-regulation isn't working properly; activating strategies are needed.

Strategies in advance

_____

_____

_____

_____

Strategies during

_____

_____

_____

_____

3. Lynn: Instructions to the entire class

Situation

In the classroom, the teacher is giving instructions, which requires everyone to listen and look at the digital whiteboard. The teacher points at things on the board and provides examples. The students have a book and notebook in front of them, which they occasionally look at. The teacher is the only one who talks and moves.

Classification

Lynn is underresponsive and passive. She needs activating strategies; Lynn isn't self-regulating to improve her concentration.

Strategies in advance

_____

_____

_____

_____

Strategies during

_____

_____

_____

_____

4. Lidy: Going home

Situation

It is the end of the day and everyone is in the corridor. All students must put on their coats, pack their things and walk down the stairs to the door leading outside. They will be picked up outside. Lidy is standing at the door of the classroom.

Classification

Lidy is overresponsive and passive. Lidy does not show self-regulation; she needs calming strategies.

Strategies in advance

_____

_____

_____

_____

Strategies during

_____

_____

_____

_____

5. Jamal: Playing football in the playground

Situation
Jamal participates in a game of football in the playground. He plays very roughly. He pushes a fellow student, who then falls and has a bleeding knee. A fight starts. The fellow student cries; he and Jamal must report to the teacher.

Classification
Jamal is underresponsive and active. He needs activating strategies; his self-regulation is too intense for his classmates.

Strategies in advance

_____

_____

_____

_____

Strategies during

_____

_____

6. Arthur: In the dressing room

Situation

Arthur is in the dressing room with his classmates, where they are getting changed for PE.

Classification

Arthur is overresponsive and active. His self-regulatory strategies are working.

Strategies in advance

_____

_____

_____

_____

Strategies during

_____

_____

_____

_____

Answers: Classifying the students through the SPI-viewing guide

1. Saadia

CLASSIFICATION

Saadia is overresponsive and active. Her self-regulation is not entirely sufficient; Saadia could use some extra calming strategies.

EXPLANATION

Saadia tries to control the situation as much as possible, so she can also control her processing of sensory input. By taking charge and dividing the tasks, Saadia ensures that she does not have to do crafts and therefore does not have to touch fabric, glue and paint. She can do the research task on her own, which she likes. For her, this means she has to deal with less sensory input. Saadia tries to further control her environment by asking other groups to be silent. The latter is of course impossible when groups are discussing and crafting. Because of this aspect and because she does not want to negotiate, she would benefit from support from the teacher to come up with better strategies.

2. Bart
CLASSIFICATION
Bart is underresponsive and active. His self-regulation isn't working properly; activating strategies are needed.

EXPLANATION
Bart is sitting still and experiences very little input, because it is quiet in the classroom and there is nothing to see. No one is moving or doing anything interesting. Bart seeks input by looking outside, moving, chewing on his pencil and fiddling with his clothes. Occasionally, he manages to read something, but Bart does not reach the level of alertness that he needs to read the entire text, to understand it and answer questions about it. He tries to get the movement he needs by walking around and going to the toilet.

3. Lynn
CLASSIFICATION
Lynn is underresponsive and passive. She needs activating strategies; Lynn isn't self-regulating to improve her concentration.

EXPLANATION
Lynn does not receive enough input to be alert. She shows no self-regulation in this situation and therefore remains a bit sleepy. Lynn looks at the digital whiteboard, the teacher and her book, but is not completely involved in what is being said. Occasionally, she responds to questions from the teacher, but she does not hold her attention for long. Lynn seems uninterested. It is difficult to get her involved in the lesson through the distance senses (hearing and sight). She also shows that she is a bit absent-minded by being clumsy. She knocks her book off the table and

the pencil follows when she attempts to stop the book from falling. Too little is going on for Lynn; there is too little sensory input to keep her alert. She is only allowed to sit still and be quiet while the teacher talks, shows things and is the only one who moves.

4. Lidy
CLASSIFICATION
Lidy is overresponsive and passive. Lidy does not show self-regulation; she needs calming strategies.

EXPLANATION
Lidy wants to be the last one out of the classroom, so as not to get stuck in the bustle near the coat racks. When she gets there, she quickly takes some things, but does not take the time to see what else she must take with her. Lidy just wants to get out of the bustle as quickly as possible. She grumbles and argues because she is tired. The sensory input has accumulated during the day. When someone touches Lidy – which is likely to happen in the corridor, at the end of the day – she responds in an irritated manner. Also having to talk to someone requires too much of her energy, so she avoids contact with the teacher at the door. She needs all her energy for the 'waterfall of input'. Once at the door, Lidy wants to go outside quickly, where there is more room. The need to go outside is stronger than wanting to comply with the rule to shake hands before you leave.

5. Jamal
CLASSIFICATION
Jamal is underresponsive and active. He needs activating strategies; his self-regulation is too intense for his classmates.

EXPLANATION
Jamal seeks input through movement. Only when he is moving a lot and fiercely, does he feel his body well. For Jamal, much and somewhat rough contact with his environment, including people, is pleasant. He does not feel the need for personal space and does not realize that others do. Jamal does not notice that he is bumping into others too roughly and that his classmates find his rough play bothersome. It is not his intention to be like that and he does not understand that others think he is being mean.

He truly hadn't noticed at all that he had knocked someone over during football. Jamal therefore does not understand why he is being called to the teacher and the accusations are coming out of the blue for him.

6. Arthur
CLASSIFICATION
Arthur is overresponsive and active. His self-regulatory strategies are working.

EXPLANATION
Arthur is overwhelmed by all sounds, movements and the chance of bodily contact that arises in a busy space. He takes care of himself by distancing himself and not responding to the stories and comments of his classmates, because this costs too much energy. Arthur needs that energy to stay afloat in the busy changing room. By making sure he's done quickly, he does not have to stay in this, for him, bothersome situation for too long. Once in the PE hall, Arthur sits down in a quiet place away from classmates who are coming in and will be running around and climbing on the already installed PE equipment.

Answers: Choose strategies
1. Saadia
STRATEGIES IN ADVANCE

- Have Saadia's group work in a quiet place in the hallway or in the library when the classroom is too hectic.
- Make reminder cards with rules of cooperation on them (for example: listen to each other, let each other finish speaking, compromise, be tolerant) and give one to each group.

STRATEGIES DURING

- Offer Saadia hearing protection during tasks that do not require group discussion.
- Offer her chewing material during discussions.
- Use the timer to show how much time there is for discussions before Saadia can start doing an individual task.

2. Bart

STRATEGIES IN ADVANCE

- Have Bart hand out the books and notebooks.
- Have Bart sharpen coloured pencils.
- Ask Bart to pick up his laminated card for that assignment and to ensure that he has everything that he needs for that assignment.

STRATEGIES DURING

- Have Bart listen to music on a music carrier.
- Ask him to do chair push-ups before every new assignment.
- Ask him to stretch after every page.
- Have Bart hand in work to you after every four assignments.

3. Lynn

STRATEGIES IN ADVANCE

- Have Lynn make the copies that are needed during the instruction.
- Ask Lynn to run up and down the stairs that she passes on her way to the copier.
- Perform jumping jacks with all students before starting the instruction.
- Make sure Lynn lays out or uses her chewable material.

STRATEGIES DURING

- Offer Lynn chewing material.
- Explain to her that she can sit down with one leg under her buttocks.
- Ask Lynn to stand up when she has to give an answer.
- Have her turn her chair around halfway through the instructions and sit astride it. Give her a sign when she should do this.

4. Lidy
STRATEGIES IN ADVANCE

- Agree in advance that Lidy will be the last to leave the classroom.
- Have Lidy shake hands in the classroom instead of in the doorway or in the hallway.
- Make sure her coat hangs in an accessible place.
- Hang a card with the jacket: 'Do I have my bag and jacket? Did I bring any extra things with me today?'

STRATEGIES DURING

- Have Lidy wait in a quiet place if her parent/guardian is not there yet.

5. Jamal
STRATEGIES IN ADVANCE

- Explain – together with Jamal – to classmates that his playing roughly is not intentional.
- Come up with a signal together, which classmates can give to Jamal when he is playing too roughly.

STRATEGIES DURING

- Ask classmates to give Jamal a sign when he is playing too roughly.
- Provide extra movement possibilities (for example, running after the ball when it rolls away from the field).

6. Arthur
Arthur is overresponsive and active. His self-regulatory strategies are working. You don't need strategies here. It is good to acknowledge what Arthur is doing and that it is working, so he realizes he is taking good care of himself. This will inspire him to look for solutions in other situations as well.

12

'He Never Does That When He's with Me'

What's this chapter about?

In this chapter we explain how your impression of a student can differ from that of a parent or colleague. We show that this may have to do with sensory processing, and especially with the sensory processing of adults interacting with the student. To help you think in the right direction, we describe the extremes of four different types of sensory processing. We use tables to show how these different types react to each other. At the end of this chapter we provide tips which you can use to reduce misunderstandings about the different impressions.

It's like they're a different child

Sometimes, during a parent–teacher conference, a parent does not recognize their child in the teacher's description or vice versa. For example, you are talking about a student who is difficult to connect with and motivate, who does not respond when you call them and regularly does not hear the instructions. You wonder if they are getting enough sleep because they are always so listless. But the parent is talking about a child who is always active at home, jumps on the trampoline or plays with their three dogs. This student is underresponsive and does not get enough input at school to build up sufficient alertness. At home, the trampoline and the pets provide enough input to keep them active.

Another possibility is that you talk about the student being cooperative and the parent talks about conflicts, irritations and a very inflexible child. This student is overresponsive and is functioning well at school because of its regime. They know where they stand and what is expected. At home, they are extremely overresponsive, because of a parent who is always enthusiastically looking for extra input. The TV is on all day and a lot of visitors stop by, who sometimes stay for dinner and sleep over, so little peace and planning are offered. The student is regularly frustrated by this and expresses their annoyances at home.

The difference in behaviour exhibited by the student also has to do with the sensory processing of the adult. The teacher or parent often decides for the child how the environment is set up, or which activities take place. Whether the adult is under- or overresponsive plays a role in this as well. You probably won't find a trampoline and three dogs at an overresponsive parent's home.

Open dialogue

These different experiences can cause misunderstandings and may result in a difficult conversation. Despite this, you all have the best intentions for the child, and it benefits the student greatly when their parent and teacher get along. This is why it is important to understand each other's view. Therefore, in this chapter, we explain to you that you are all talking about the same child. But, as we just mentioned, the child's reaction also has to do with the adult's sensory processing. The different impressions may depend on the type of adult the child is dealing with. Being aware of this can help you start a different conversation about the student.

How do you get to know each other?

First, you must know what type the student is. If all has gone well, you now have enough knowledge to classify them. To find out what type of adult the student is dealing with, in this chapter we will first take a look at the home situation. We'll show you that there are four types of parent. If you have no idea what the home situation is like, you can find out by asking the parent three questions. You can then use a table to look up how the parent and the child match up. Then, we will look at your type; you can look up your match with the student in the last table. To complete the picture, we put all parties in this table: the student, the parent and the teacher. You can now see all combinations in one glance.

We are aware that looking at what type of sensory-seeker you are for the first time can be complicated or confrontational. This is especially true for parents who do not have your prior knowledge. That is why we want to emphasize that all the types we outline are exaggerated. This way, you get to know the extremes, and with this knowledge and practice you can start to recognize nuances. We hope that this information helps you get more insight and work together more easily.

The home situation

If you do not have the same picture of a student as the parent, you can investigate whether the parent is mainly under- or overresponsive and whether the parent is actively trying to influence the environmental input or not. This is often clearly visible when wearing your SPI-Glasses. We will further elaborate on this below for several aspects of the household. Wearing our SPI-Glasses, we provide examples of what a household can look like with one dominant form of sensory processing. We assume that one type predominates: that the person who takes care of the child and does the housekeeping most of the time will predominate in terms of what kind of household there is. The points we describe, such as housekeeping, visitors and sounds, have been chosen because of their impact on the child.

Characteristics of the four types of parent

Underresponsive and active
(Characteristics: lively, spontaneous, boisterous/chaotic, asks for a lot of attention, goes on and on and on)

This parent is mostly underresponsive and seeks extra sensory input.

THE HOUSEHOLD IS FLEXIBLE; THE PARENT:
- Likes spontaneous actions: 'We were supposed to go to the cinema, but the weather is so nice – we'll go cycling!'
- Does laundry sometimes on Saturday, sometimes on Thursday evening or not for a whole week, and dinner time changes constantly.
- Goes grocery shopping at different times and without a list.
- Keeps things less organized, so objects are not always in the same place.
- Can be flexible with rules, for example as a general rule, eight o'clock is bedtime, but it can also be half past eight.

VISITORS; THE PARENT:
- Loves to have many visitors, the more the merrier.
- Enjoys it when a guest stays for dinner at the last minute and everyone is welcome to stay overnight.

SOUNDS; THE PARENT:
- Likes to allow sounds, for example from the TV or radio.
- Doesn't find hearing musical instrument practice a problem.

MORNING ROUTINE; THE PARENT:
- Pays attention to the clothes the children are wearing and intervenes if something isn't right, like if the combination of items doesn't look good.
- Is preparing breakfast following the latest food trends, while the radio plays. One week, it's a goji berry smoothie, the next week, oatmeal porridge.

WHAT IS TRICKY? THE PARENT:
- Finds it difficult to align routines with the child's needs. The parent is more likely to expect the opposite; the child must adapt to the routine of the parent.
- Gets irritated faster when it's quiet. Becomes cranky and impatient.

Underresponsive and passive
(Characteristics: flexible and sluggish, isn't easily disturbed, misses information, hard to reach)

This parent is mostly underresponsive and doesn't seek extra sensory input.

THE HOUSEHOLD IS CALM; THE PARENT:
- Must be regularly reminded of household chores.
- Does laundry when there are no more clean clothes. Removes clothing from the drying rack to put on immediately.
- Does groceries when the fridge is empty, without a list.
- Does not tidy much; it is a bit messy and things are not where they should be.
- Has no clear rules. The child goes to bed when they are tired.

VISITORS; THE PARENT:
- Doesn't plan for many visitors themselves, but people are always welcome.
- Finds it no problem if a guest joins dinner last minute.

SOUNDS; THE PARENT:
- Allows more sounds, for example from TV or radio; does not always turn these on themselves.
- Doesn't find hearing musical instrument practice a problem.

MORNING ROUTINE; THE PARENT:
- Has no fixed routine.
- Forgets things regularly, even when those things were prepared to be ready to take along.

WHAT IS TRICKY? THE PARENT:
- Isn't bothered by others, therefore has less need to oversee or arrange their activities and therefore doesn't notice the needs of others.
- Retreats if too much is asked, if they cannot meet all demands. Avoids contact when this happens.

Overresponsive and active
(Characteristics: structured and decisive, eye for detail, gets tense easily, wants to be in control)

This parent is predominantly overresponsive and actively tries to influence sensory input.

HOUSEHOLD IS STRUCTURED; THE PARENT:
- Tries to maintain a structured and controlled household. Because the parent is not alone, this doesn't always work.
- Has a fixed place for everything, knows where everything is.
- Does the laundry at a fixed time and in a fixed order. Colours on Tuesday, whites on Friday. Irons everything and makes neat stacks in the wardrobe.
- Keeps a shopping list. Ensures that it is written down in the order in which the items are found in the store.
- Has clear rules and tasks. There is no deviation from the set bedtime.

VISITORS; THE PARENT:
- Is happy when visitors come by on appointment, with clear intentions: we are going to drink coffee, or you're coming over for a nice barbecue.
- Prefers a limited number of visitors at a time.

SOUNDS; THE PARENT:
- Can handle sounds, but preferably not mixed up and not when they are trying to focus on something.
- Doesn't mind musical instrument practice at fixed, agreed to times, behind a closed door. Toys with sound are played with behind a closed door too.

MORNING ROUTINE; THE PARENT:
- Follows a fixed routine. Everyone receives directions about what needs to be done and where everything can be found.
- Doesn't ever forget anything; some things have already been lying in a visible place for a few days.

WHAT IS TRICKY? THE PARENT:
- Is quickly bothered by others, therefore has a need to oversee or arrange their activities.
- Is quickly irritated by unexpected events, will complain and accuse.

Overresponsive and passive
(Characteristics: sensitive, perceptive, likes quiet, nervous, can suddenly get upset)

This parent is predominantly overresponsive and tries to exert little influence on sensory input.

THE HOUSEHOLD IS CALM; THE PARENT:
- Prefers to do household chores alone; this means consultation or explanation (how to do everything exactly) will not be necessary.
- Has their own system in which everything has a fixed place, but if someone else moves it, it won't be put back in that place.
- Makes a basic shopping list but is quickly distracted by offers and new products when shopping.
- Does laundry in stages. For example, washing and hanging it to dry one time, folding and ironing the next.
- Doesn't have clear rules and tasks. The child sometimes goes to bed early, because the parent needs some peace and quiet.

VISITORS; THE PARENT:
- Is happy when visitors come by on appointment, but preferably not every day.
- Feels more comfortable with one-on-one visits than at parties.

SOUNDS; THE PARENT:
- Grumbles about sounds (loud talking, laughter, musical instruments, toys).
- Does not turn on the radio or TV as background noise.

MORNING ROUTINE; THE PARENT:
- Has a routine in mind, but is not clear about it to the other family members.
- Realizes at night that the things for the school trip aren't ready yet and gets up to organize this.

WHAT IS TRICKY? THE PARENT:
- Is quickly bothered by others, grumbles about that.
- Sets strict (sometimes too strict) rules when something goes wrong (which causes them to be overresponsive).

Three questions

Perhaps bells have started ringing while reading the descriptions above and you now have an idea about which type a certain parent is predominantly. If this isn't the case, we will take you another step with a number of questions for you to ask the parent.

The parent's answers provide information about their sensory preferences and as such about the parent's sensory processing.

	Parent is actively underresponsive	Parent is passively underresponsive	Parent is actively overresponsive	Parent is passively overresponsive
How do you prefer breakfast on weekends?	We usually bake croissants or something else and we all sit at the table together. Then, we discuss what we will be doing that day.	It doesn't really matter; sometimes at 10:00, sometimes not until 11:00. It's different every weekend. Sometimes we have breakfast together, sometimes separately. Sometimes at home, sometimes in a café.	At 10:00, the table is already set. Everyone has their own role in preparing breakfast. I take care of the sandwich toppings. Everyone gets a tasty egg. I always boil eggs for five minutes, so they're not overcooked, yet also not too runny.	Everyone is doing their own thing at the breakfast table. I usually read the paper.
How do you celebrate your child's birthday?	Everyone is invited, we all play adventurous games and we have a different theme every year.	He usually brings it up himself, tells us whom he wants to invite and what we could do or where we could go. And that's fine by me.	He is allowed to invite eight friends and we usually have the party somewhere where everything is arranged for us. This way, I don't have the mess at home. I do bring earplugs.	He comes up with all kinds of ideas and then we arrange something. I appreciate it when other parents help, and I always hope that not too many children show up.
Can you describe your child's room?	Cosy, with lots of toys, a bed that can be used to build forts and on which you can jump.	His room is fine, but I don't go there that often. I think he cleans it up a bit himself.	I got those handy storage bins so he can see exactly where his toys need to go. But I really have to push him to get him to actually tidy up.	Sometimes it's a mess and I can't find anything, but I don't go there that often. Twice a week to put away clean laundry.

The effects of different types of parent on the child

Just like the student, the parent can predominantly be a certain type: under- or overresponsive, active or passive. An overresponsive parent and an overresponsive child often go well together because they have the same needs: little sensory input and regular moments of peace and quiet. But an overresponsive student who has an underresponsive parent, a parent who in this case seeks extra sensory input, will have a harder time at home. The overresponsive child is looking for peace and quiet at home. But home is often a bit tumultuous, because that is what the parent prefers.

Now that you have a good impression of the predominant types for the student and parent, you can look them up in the table below and see how they match. This allows you to better understand why the parent describes their child in a certain way. At the top of the table, you will find the student type, and on the left, the parent type.

Student → Parent →	Actively underresponsive	Passively underresponsive	Actively overresponsive	Passively overresponsive
Actively underresponsive	☺ Parent and child are sensory seekers; their needs and actions correspond. ☺ The child happily participates in seeking sensory input. The parent responds positively to the child's ideas.	☺ The parent is a sensory seeker. In the process, they make noise, unexpected things happen, and there is a lot of activity. The child benefits from this; they are sufficiently activated.	☹ The parent is a sensory seeker, which can make the home situation quite hectic. After a day of sensory overload in school, this child might collapse when they get home, because there is not much peace and quiet to be found there either. ☹ The child is bothered by the parent. ☹ The parent offers insufficient planning and peace and quiet. The child, needing this, must look for it themselves.	☹ The parent is a sensory seeker, which can make the home situation quite hectic. The extra sensory input at home can quickly become too much for this child. ☹ The parent is too hectic for the child. The child is bothered by this, but doesn't avoid sensory input and/ or look for peace and quiet themselves.

Passively underresponsive	☺ The child is a sensory seeker. This fits perfectly; the extra sensory input added by the child is pleasant for the parent as well. The parent is activated by the child's behaviour.	☺ Parent and child fit well together; they have the same needs. ☹ The parent generates little extra sensory input. The child can't function independently well, because they don't build up sufficient alertness to be able to focus properly. They have to be reminded of what they are supposed to do many times. In general, the child doesn't reach the level of alertness necessary to function properly.	☺ Parent and child fit well together. The parent does not generate extra sensory input, which is pleasant for the child. ☹ The child's need for less sensory input is not noticed by the parent.	☺ Parent and child fit well together. The parent does not generate extra sensory input, which is pleasant for the child. ☹ The child's need for less sensory input is not noticed by the parent.
Actively overresponsive	☺ The parent tries to limit sensory input and tries to create peace and quiet, while the child seeks extra sensory input and can create commotion in doing so. This will particularly bother the parent, the child not so much. The parent experiences the child as very hectic and will try to calm them down. Meanwhile, the child needs this activity to function.	☹ The parent limits the amount of sensory input, so the child doesn't build up sufficient alertness. The inactivity does not stand out; the parent benefits from a quiet child. The child is insufficiently activated.	☺ Parent and child understand each other's need to control the amount of sensory input. Both try to create a planned environment. ☺ The child's strategies are accepted because the parent will recognize them as calming. ☹ Parent and child both suffer from too much sensory input and may both be irritated, which can aggravate the situation.	☺ Planning and peace and quiet prevail: a good situation for the child who does not regulate sensory input themselves. The parent does this for them. The child is in an environment that works well for them.

cont.

Student → Parent ↓	Actively underresponsive	Passively underresponsive	Actively overresponsive	Passively overresponsive
Passively overresponsive	☹ The parent is sensitive to sensory input and the child generates a lot of sensory input. The parent can experience the child as being too hectic, and this can bother them. This may result in irritation and frustration from the parent.	☹ The parent benefits from the inactivity – and thus the relative peace and quiet – of the child. The child does not take sufficient action.	☺ The parent understands the child's request for a planned environment. The parent needs this too and understands the child's avoidant strategies as well.	☺ Parent and child have the same needs. Both are quickly bothered by their environment, so the parent understands the child.

Matching teacher and student

You too, with your way of processing sensory input, have a certain influence on the student. For example, if you yourself are underresponsive and are therefore adding a lot of sensory input, this is fine for the underresponsive student who does not look for sensory input themselves. You both love choosing the drums for the music lesson.

We have put on the SPI-Glasses and looked at the types of teachers, based on a number of lesson situations. We have chosen aspects of teaching that have clear consequences for the student. Again: extremes are described here – none of the described types really exist. Where do you fit best?

Characteristics of the four types of teacher

Underresponsive and active
(Lively, spontaneous, boisterous/chaotic, asks for a lot of attention, goes on and on and on)

This teacher is mostly underresponsive and looking for sensory input.

- Way of presenting
  - Is enthusiastic, intense, louder than average, with a lot of energy.
  - Does unexpected things.
- Rules, order and planning
  - Is spontaneous, often looking for new ideas.
  - Cares less about routine and rules – sometimes follows them, sometimes doesn't.
  - Believes enthusiasm is more important than order.
  - Regularly deviates from the planning.
- Personal attention for and participation of students
  - Notices the needs of students less.
  - Has many ideas of their own; there is little room for participation.

Underresponsive and passive
(Flexible and sluggish, isn't easily disturbed, misses information, hard to reach)

This teacher is mostly underresponsive and does not seek extra sensory input.

- Way of presenting
  - Is calm, monotonous, consistent in tone and energy.
  - Follows the existing lesson plans.
- Rules, order and planning
  - Is flexible.
  - Cares less about routine and rules, but does usually follow them.
  - Isn't quickly bothered by things; the classroom can be a bit noisier.
  - Does not have a good grip on long-term planning.
- Personal attention for and participation of students
  - Isn't quick to notice things; may therefore miss signals from students.
  - Gives students a lot of freedom to be themselves; there is a high level of student involvement in decision making.

Overresponsive and active
(Structured and decisive, eye for detail, gets tense easily, wants to be in control)

This teacher is predominantly overresponsive and actively tries to influence sensory input.

- Way of presenting
  - Stays away from emotions to keep calm.
  - Gives a lot of clues about what is important to watch out for.
- Rules, order and planning
  - Likes rules, is inflexible.
  - Likes routine and creates a fixed planning. Loves repeating the same activities.
  - Wants order in their class.
  - Strictly follows the (long-term) planning.
- Personal attention for and participation of students
  - Notices everything, is quick to comprehend, quickly connects things.
  - Assumes they already know the students' needs; there is little room for participation.

Overresponsive and passive
(Sensitive, perceptive, likes quiet, nervous, can suddenly get upset)

This teacher is predominantly overresponsive and tries to exert little influence on sensory input.

- Way of presenting
  - Responds to all that is happening in class; can therefore be somewhat chaotic.
  - Gives short, intense presentations.
- Rules, order and planning
  - Is flexible but does not oversee the consequences.
  - Responds to the needs of the students; regularly adjusts rules and routines accordingly.
  - Loves order, peace and structure; doesn't put this into action as much themselves.
  - Regularly forgets to follow the planning because of the issues of the day.
- Personal attention for and participation of students
  - Notices everything; can tell how the student is feeling from a single gesture or facial expression.
  - Follows the needs of students; there is a lot of room for student involvement in decision-making.

 The effects of different types of parent and teacher on the student

Now, you can use your knowledge about the student, the parent and yourself, to look at the following table and see what the consequences are for the student in different situations at school and at home. Here, the teacher type has been incorporated in the table as well. This gives you a quick overview of the school and home situation and whether they differ in terms of types of adult. This allows you to discover why you may have a very different image of a student than their parent does.

Student ⟶	Actively underresponsive	Passively underresponsive	Actively overresponsive	Passively overresponsive
Parent Actively underresponsive	☺ Parent and child are sensory seekers; their needs and actions correspond. ☺ The child happily participates in seeking sensory input. The parent responds positively to the child's ideas.	☺ The parent is a sensory seeker. In the process, they make noise, unexpected things happen and there is a lot of activity. The child benefits from this; they are sufficiently activated.	☹ The parent is a sensory seeker, which can make the home situation quite hectic. After a day of sensory overload in school, this child might collapse when they get home, because there is not much peace and quiet to be found there either. ☹ The child is bothered by the parent. ☹ The parent offers insufficient planning and peace and quiet. The child, needing this, must look for it themselves.	☹ The parent is a sensory seeker, which can make the home situation quite hectic. The extra sensory input at home can quickly become too much for this child. ☹ The parent is too hectic for the child. The child is bothered by this, but doesn't avoid sensory input and/or look for peace and quiet themselves.

Teacher Actively underresponsive	☺ Teacher and student are sensory seekers; their needs and actions correspond. ☺ The student happily participates in seeking sensory input. The teacher responds positively to the student's ideas.	☺ The teacher is a sensory seeker. In the process, they make noise, unexpected things happen, and there is a lot of activity. The student benefits from this; they are sufficiently activated.	☺ The teacher is a sensory seeker, so the classroom can be hectic. There may not be enough peace and quiet in this class for the student. ☹ The student is bothered by this teacher. ☹ The teacher offers insufficient planning and peace and quiet. The student needing this, must look for it themselves.	☺ The teacher is a sensory seeker, so the classroom can be hectic. The extra sensory input in the classroom can quickly become too much for this student. ☹ The teacher is too hectic for the student. The student is bothered by this, but doesn't avoid sensory input and/or look for peace and quiet themselves.
Parent Passively underresponsive	☺ The child is a sensory seeker. This fits perfectly; the extra sensory input added by the child is pleasant for the parent as well. The parent is activated by the child's behaviour.	☺ Parent and child fit well together; they have the same needs. ☹ The parent generates little extra sensory input. The child can't function independently well, because they don't build up sufficient alertness to be able to focus properly. They have to be reminded of what they are supposed to do many times. In general, the child doesn't reach the level of alertness necessary to function properly.	☺ Parent and child fit well together. The parent does not generate extra sensory input, which is pleasant for the child. ☹ The child's need for less sensory input is not noticed by the parent.	☺ Parent and child fit well together. The parent does not generate extra sensory input, which is pleasant for the child. ☹ The child's need for less sensory input is not noticed by the parent.

cont.

Student →	Actively underresponsive	Passively underresponsive	Actively overresponsive	Passively overresponsive
Teacher **Passively underresponsive**	☺ The student is a sensory seeker. This fits perfectly; the extra sensory input added by the student is pleasant for the teacher as well. The teacher is activated by the student's behaviour.	☺ Teacher and student fit well together; they have the same needs. ☹ The teacher generates little extra sensory input. The student can't function independently well, because they don't build up sufficient alertness to be able to focus properly. They have to be reminded of what they are supposed to do many times. In general, the student doesn't reach the level of alertness needed to function properly.	☺ Teacher and student fit well together. The teacher does not generate extra sensory input, which is pleasant for the student. ☹ The student's need for less sensory input is not noticed by the teacher.	☺ Teacher and student fit well together. The teacher does not generate extra sensory input, which is pleasant for the student. ☹ The student's need for less sensory input is not noticed by the teacher.
Parent **Actively overresponsive**	☺ The parent tries to limit sensory input and tries to create peace and quiet, while the child seeks extra sensory input and can create commotion in doing so. This will particularly bother the parent, the child not so much. The parent experiences the child as very hectic and will try to calm them down. Meanwhile, the child needs this activity to function.	☹ The parent limits the amount of sensory input, so the child doesn't build up sufficient alertness. The inactivity does not stand out; the parent benefits from a quiet child. The child is insufficiently activated.	☺ Parent and child understand each other's need to control the amount of sensory input. Both try to create a planned environment. ☺ The child's strategies are accepted because the parent will recognize them as calming. ☹ Parent and child both suffer from too much sensory input and may both be irritated, which can aggravate the situation.	☺ Planning and peace and quiet prevail: a good situation for the child who does not regulate sensory input themselves. The parent does this for them. The child is in an environment that works well for them.

Teacher Actively overresponsive	☺ This teacher tries to limit sensory input and tries to create peace and quiet, while the student seeks extra sensory input and can create commotion in doing so. This will particularly bother the teacher, the student not so much. The teacher experiences the student as very hectic and will try to calm them down. Meanwhile, the student needs this activity to function.	☹ The teacher limits the amount of sensory input, so the student doesn't build up sufficient alertness. The inactivity does not stand out; the teacher benefits from a calm student. The student is insufficiently activated.	☺ Teacher and student understand each other's need to control the amount of sensory input. Both try to create a planned environment. ☺ The student's strategies are accepted because the teacher will recognize them as calming. ☹ Teacher and student both suffer from too much sensory input and may both be irritated, which can aggravate the situation.	☺ Planning and peace and quiet prevail: a good situation for the student who does not regulate sensory input themselves. The teacher does that for them. The student is in an environment that works well for them.
Parent Passively overresponsive	☹ The parent is sensitive to sensory input and the child generates a lot of sensory input. The parent can experience the child as being too hectic, and this can bother them. This may result in irritation and frustration from the parent.	☹ The parent benefits from the inactivity – and thus the relative peace and quiet – of the child. The child does not take sufficient action.	☺ The parent understands the child's request for a planned environment. The parent needs this too and understands the child's avoidant strategies as well.	☺ Parent and child have the same needs. Both are quickly bothered by their environment, so the parent understands the child.

cont.

Student →	Actively underresponsive	Passively underresponsive	Actively overresponsive	Passively overresponsive
Teacher **Passively overresponsive**	☹ The teacher is sensitive to sensory input and the student generates a lot of sensory input. The teacher may experience the student as being too hectic and this can bother them. This may result in irritation and frustration from the teacher.	☹ The teacher benefits from the inactivity – and thus the relative peace and quiet – of the student. The student does not take sufficient action.	☺ The teacher understands the student's request for a planned environment. The teacher needs this too and understands the student's avoidant strategies as well.	☺ Teacher and student have the same needs. Both are quickly bothered by their environment, so the teacher understands the student.

Tips to reduce lack of understanding

When you notice that you and the parent see the student very differently, you can discuss this with the help of the information above. Explain what your impression is based on, and emphasize what the student themselves is already doing about their behaviour and how this shows skill on their part. Although the types of parent are extremes and do not exist in real life, looking at the table with them can be a sensitive issue.

- Tell the parent about the student:
  - what you have noticed in class
  - whether you are thinking of under- or overresponsivity in the student and why
  - which strategies the student is displaying themselves
  - which strategies you offer in addition
  - which strategies you use with the entire class.
- Introduce the Fan-model and explain what the student thinks their sensory need is in the classroom.
- Consider, together with the parent, whether the student could also do this at home.
- Show some strategies that the student uses in the classroom. There are probably some strategies among these which can also be used at home, such as:
  - dining room chair push-ups
  - chewing material while watching TV or during transitions
  - fidgeting while visiting the supermarket.
- Provide tips to use when out and about as well, which can be found in Chapter 6.

Bibliography

Allen, A.P., Jacob, T.J.C. & Smith, A.P. (2014) 'Effects and after-effects of chewing gum on vigilance, heart rate, EEG and mood.' *Physiology & Behavior 133*, 22, 244–251.

Andrade, J. (2010) 'What does doodling do?' *Applied Cognitive Psychology 24*, 1, 100–106.

Anthes, E. (2010) 'It's SO LOUD, I can't hear my budget!' *Psychology Today*. Accessed on 08 April 2015 at https://www.psychologytoday.com/articles/201010/outside-in-its-so-loud-i-cant-hear-my-budget.

Arnold, A.J., Winkielman, P. & Dobkins, K. (2019) 'Interoception and Social Connection.' *Frontiers in Psychology*. Accessed on 06 July 2021 at https://www.frontiersin.org/articles/10.3389/fpsyg.2019.02589/full.

Bailer, D.S. & Miller, L.J. (2011) *No Longer a Secret: Unique Common Sense Strategies for Children with Sensory Motor Challenges*. Arlington, TX: Future Horizons.

Barrett, L.F., Quigley, K.S., Bliss-Moreau, E. & Aronson, K.R. (2004) 'Interoceptive sensitivity and self-reports of emotional experience.' *Journal of Personality and Social Psychology 87*(5), 684–697.

Best, J.R. (2012) 'Exergaming immediately enhances children's executive function.' *Developmental Psychology 48*, 5, 1501–1510.

Bird, G. & Cook, R. (2013) 'Mixed emotions: The contribution of alexithymia to the emotional symptoms of autism.' *Transl. Psychiatry 3*, e285.

Brewer, R., Cook, R. & Bird, G. (2016) 'Alexithymia: A general deficit of interoception.' *R. Soc. open sci 3*, 150664.

Bunce, D.M., Flens, E.A. & Neiles, K.Y. (2010) 'How long can students pay attention in class? A study of student attention decline using clickers.' *Journal of Chemical Education 87*, 1438–1443.

Cain, W.S. & Johnson, F. Jr. (1978) 'Lability of odor pleasantness: Influence of mere exposure.' *Perception 7*, 459–465.

Cardon, G., Clercq, D. de, Bourdeaudhuij, I. & Breithecker, D. (2004) 'Sitting habits in elementary schoolchildren: A traditional versus a "Moving School".' *Patient Education and Counseling 54*, 2, 133–142.

Cowley, S. (2010) *Lesgeven voor Dummies. [Teaching Skills for Dummies.]* Amsterdam: Pearson Education Benelux.

Craig, A.D. (2002) 'How do you feel? Interoception: The sense of the physiological condition of the body.' *Nature Reviews. Neuroscience, 3*, 8, 655–666.

Craig, A.D. (2003) 'Interoception: The sense of the physiological condition of the body.' *Current Opinion in Neurobiology 13*, 4, 500–505.

Dalgliesh, C. (2014) *Overprikkeld: praktische strategieën om de wereld van je prikkelgevoelige kind te structureren. [The Sensory Child Gets Organized.]* Amsterdam: Hogrefe Uitgevers.

Drolette, E.S., Scuddle, M.R., Raine, L.B., Davis Moore, R., Saliba, B.J., Pontifex, M.B. & Hillman, C.H. (2014) 'Acute exercise facilitates brain function and cognition in children who need it most: An ERP study of individual differences in inhibitory control capacity.' *Developmental Cognitive Neuroscience 7*, 53–64.

Dukette, D. & Cornish, D. (2009) *The Essential 20: Twenty Components of an Excellent Health Care Team.* Pittsburgh, PA: Dorrance Publishing.

Dunn, W. (2013) *Living Sensationally: Understanding Your Senses.* London: Jessica Kingsley Publishers.

Ebbens, S. & Ettekoven, S. (2013) *Samenwerkend leren. [Co-operative Learning.]* Groningen: Noordhoff Uitgevers.

Farley, J., Evan, F.R. & Kingstone, A. (2013) 'Everyday attention and lecture retention: The effect of time, fidgeting and mind wandering.' *Frontiers in Psychology 4,* 619.

Fedewa, A.L. & Ahn, S. (2011) 'The effects of physical activity and physical fitness on children's achievement and cognitive outcomes: A meta-analysis.' *Research Quarterly for Exercise and Sport 82,* 3, 521–535.

Feldman Barret, L. (2017) *How Emotions Are Made: The Secret Life of the Brain.* London: Pan Books.

Fisher, V., Godwin, K.E. & Seltman, H. (2014) 'Visual environment, attention allocation, and learning in young children: When too much of a good thing may be bad.' *Psychological Science 25,* 7, 1362–1370.

Frank, D.A., Klass, P.E., Earls, F. & Eisenberg, L. (1996) 'Infants and young children in orphanages: One view from pediatrics and child psychiatry.' *Pediatrics 97,* 569–578.

Golden, R.N., Gaynes, B.N., Ekstrom, R.D., Hamer, R.M., Jacobsen, F.M., Suppes, T., Wisner, K.L. & Nemeroff, C.B. (2005) 'The efficacy of light therapy in the treatment of mood disorders: A review and meta-analysis of the evidence.' *American Journal of Psychiatry 162,* 4, 656–662.

Hannaford, C. (2005) *Smart Moves: Why Learning Is Not All in Your Head.* Salt Lake City, UT: Great River Books.

Hattie, J. (2013) *Visible Learning: A Synthesis of over 800 Meta-Analyses Relating to Achievement.* London: Routledge.

Heijden, I. van der, Hoog, R. de & Stultiens-Houben, S. (2012) *Prikkels in de Groep: Samenwerken aan een sensorisch waardevolle omgeving voor kinderen en jongeren met een verstandelijke beperking. [Sensations in the Group: Working Together on a Sensory Valuable Environment for Mentally Impaired Children and Adolescents.]* Apeldoorn: Uitgeverij Garant.

Hinckson, E.A., Aminian, S., Ikeda, E., Stewart, T., Oliver, M., Duncan, S. & Schofield, G. (2013) 'Acceptability of standing workstations in elementary schools: A pilot study.' *Preventive Medicine 56,* 1, 82–85.

Hoogeveen, P. & Winkels, J. (2001) *Het Didactische Werkvormenboek. Variatie en differentiatie in de praktijk. [The Book on Didactic Teaching Methods. Variation and Differentiation in Practice.]* Assen: Koninklijke van Gorcum.

Horeweg, A. (2018) *De Traumasensitieve School. Anders kijken naar gedrag. [The Traumasensitive School: A Different View on Problem Behaviour in the Classroom.]* Tielt: Uitgeverij Lannoo.

Hupperets, M.D.W., Verhagen, E.A.L.M. & van Mechelen, W. (2009) 'Effect on unsupervised home based proprioceptive training on recurrences of ankle sprain: Randomised controlled trial.' *British Medical Journal 339,* b2684.

Jarrett, O.S., Maxwell, D.M., Dickerson, C., Hoge, P., Davies, G. & Yetley, A. (1998) 'Impact of recess on classroom behavior: Group effects and individual differences.' *The Journal of Educational Research 92,* 2, 121–126.

Jonas, P.M. (2009) *Laughing and Learning: An Alternative to Shut Up and Listen.* Lanham, MD: Rowman and Littlefield Education.

Kandasamy, N., Garfinkel, S.N., Page, L., Hardy, B., Critchley, H.D., Gurnell, M. & Coates, J.M. (2016) 'Interoceptive ability predicts survival on a London trading floor.' *Scientific Report 6,* art. nr. 32986. Accessed on 23 March 2021 at www.ncbi.nlm.nih.gov/pmc/articles/PMC5027524.

Karnath, H.O. & Broetz, D. (2003) 'Understanding and treating "Pusher Syndrome".' *Physical Therapy 83,* 12, 1119–1125.

Kranowitz, C. (2007) *The Out-of-Sync Child: Recognizing & Coping with Sensory Processing Disorder.* Arlington, TX: Future Horizons.

Kurihara, K. (2009) 'Glutamate: From discovery as a food flavor to role as a basic taste (umami).' *The American Journal of Clinical Nutrition 90,* 3, 719S–722S.

Langelaan, T. & Plomp, W. (2004) *De Excellente Leerkracht. De fundamenten van zijn succes. [The Excellent Teacher: Fundamentals of Their Success.]* Amsterdam: Uitgeverij Nelissen.

Mahar, M.T., Murphy, S.K., Rowe, D.A., Golden, J., Shields, A.T. & Raedeke, T.D. (2006) 'Effects of a classroom-based program on physical activity and on-task behavior.' *Medicine & Science in Sports & Exercise 38*, 12, 2086–2094.

Mahler, K.J. (2017) *Interoception: The Eighth Sensory System. Practical Solutions for Improving Self-Regulation, Self-Awareness and Social Understanding.* Buchanan, MI: AAPC.

Miller, L.J. (2006) *Sensational Kids: Hope and Help for Children with Sensory Processing Disorder (SPD).* New York: Perigee.

Mohiyeddini, C. & Semple, S. (2013) 'Displacement behaviour regulates the experience of stress in men.' *Stress 16*, 2, 163–171.

Moncrieff, R.W. (1966) *Odour Preferences.* Hoboken, NJ: John Wiley & Sons.

Morgan, K., Johnson, A.J. & Miles, C. (2014) 'Chewing gum moderates the vigilance decrement.' *British Journal of Psychology 105*, 2, 214–225.

Moyer, C.A., Rounds, J. & Hannum, J.W. (2004) 'A meta-analysis of massage therapy research.' *Psychological Bulletin 130*, 1, 3–18.

Mullender-Wijnsma, M.J., Hartman, E., Greef, J.W. de, Doolaard, S., Bosker, R.J. & Visscher, C. (2016) 'Physically active math and language lessons improve academic achievement: A cluster randomized controlled trial.' *Pediatrics 137*, 1–9.

Parker, C.B. (2015) 'Embracing stress is more important than reducing stress, Stanford psychologist says.' Accessed on 13 March 2021 at https://news.stanford.edu/2015/05/07/stress-embrace-mcgonigal-050715.

Pedersen, P.M., Wandel, A., Jørgensen, H.S., Nakavama, H., Raaschou, H.O. & Olson, T.S. (1996) 'Ipsilateral pushing in stroke: Incidence, relation to neuropsychological symptoms, and impact on rehabilitation – the Copenhagen Stroke Study.' *Archives of Physical Medicine and Rehabilitation 77*, 25–28.

Porges, S.W. (2008) 'The polyvagal perspective.' *Biological Psychology 74*, 2, 116–143.

Porges, S.W. (2011) *The Polyvagal Theory: Neuro-Physiological Foundations of Emotions, Attachment, Communication, Self-Regulation.* New York: W.W. Norton.

Saarikallio, S. (2011) 'Music as emotional self-regulation throughout adulthood.' *Psychology of Music 39*, 3, 307–327.

Schilling, D.L., Washington, K., Billingsley, F.F. & Deitz, J. (2003) 'Classroom seating for children with Attention Deficit Hyperactivity Disorder: Therapy balls versus chairs.' *American Journal of Occupational Therapy 57*, 534–541.

Sibley, B.A. & Etnier, J.L. (2003) 'The relationship between physical activity and cognition in children: A meta-analysis.' *Pediatric Exercise Science 15*, 243–256.

Siegel, D.J. (1999) *The Developing Mind: Toward a Neurobiology of Interpersonal Experience.* New York: Guilford Press.

Thoonsen, M. & van der Gaag, M. (2021) 'Wiebelen en friemelen voor mensen met een verstandelijke beperking. Over de invloed van zintuiglijke prikkelverwerking op (be)leven.' ['Sensory solutions for mentally disabled people. About the influence of sensory processing on experiencing life.']. Huizen: Uitgeverij Pica.

Torbeyns, T., Bailey, S., Bos, I. & Meeusen, R. (2014) 'Active workstations to fight sedentary behavior.' *Sports Medicine 44*, 9, 1261–1273.

Umeda, S., Tochizawa, S., Shibata, M. & Terasawa, Y. (2016) 'Prospective memory mediated by interoceptive accuracy: A psychophysiological approach.' *Philosophical Transactions of the Royal Society*, B 371, 20160005.

Veiligheid.nl (n.d.) 'Enkelblessures door sport.' ['Ankle injuries caused by sports.'] Accessed on 01 July 2021 at www.veiligheid.nl/cijfers/enkelblessures-door-sport.

de Vos, T. (2010) 'Smaakontwikkeling bij zeer jonge kinderen.' ['Taste development in very young children.'] Accessed on 08 April 2015 at www.opvoedadvies.nl/smaakontwikkeling.htm.

de Vree, J. (n.d.) 'Trap.' Accessed on 01 July 2021 at www.joostdevree.nl/shtmls/trap.shtml.

de Waard, H. & King, D. (2000) *Tips voor Lesgevers. Suggesties voor meer werkplezier. [Tips for Teachers: Suggestions for Having More Fun at Work.]* Apeldoorn: Garant.

Wedekind, C., Seebeck, T., Bettens, F. & Paepke, J. (1995) 'MHC-dependent mate preferences in humans.' *Biological Sciences 260*, 1359, 245–249.

Wilson, K. & Korn, J.H. (2007) 'Attention during lectures: Beyond ten minutes.' *Teaching of Psychology 34*, 2, 85–89.

Appendix 1: Further Research

Investigating sensory processing

It may be the case that the teacher, supervisor and/or parent thinks that sensory processing causes a lot of problems for a student and that there are so many difficulties, that the student is not able to cope well at school and at home. Further investigating and testing is advisable to see whether this behaviour is (partly) the result of problematic sensory processing. This evaluation must be done by a specialist who has followed training for sensory processing and is certified in this subject. This is usually an occupational, physical or speech therapist.

SPD therapists conduct evaluations through conversations with the child, parents and teachers and through observation of the child. The therapists can use a standardized questionnaire, for instance the 'Sensory Profile' or the 'School Companion'. The Sensory Profile is for people of different ages and is aimed at the home situation. The School Companion, for children aged three to 12, is entirely focused on the situation at school. The results of the evaluation show which problems there may be with sensory processing. This makes it clear what effect sensory processing has on daily functioning. The aforementioned questionnaires are not intended to make a diagnosis. It is, however, a good, complementary tool for formulating practical advice.

Based on all the information gathered about sensory processing, the child, the parent and the teacher discuss with the therapist which strategies can help. These strategies fit within the daily routine of the child and are given as a kind of homework. These strategies can be tried out at home, at school and in other places. After all, the child has to learn how to deal with their sensory input in daily life, because that is where adjustments have to be made. The therapist guides this process.

Appendix 2: Additional Information

Our services

On our website www.DutchSensorySolutions.com you will find extensive information about sensory processing, videos, downloads and links.

We offer face-to-face and online training and would love to hear from you if you have any questions on sensory processing or this book or maybe would like to discuss one of your students.

Index

Other JKP books

Simple Stuff to Get Kids Self-Regulating in School

Awesome and In Control Lesson Plans, Worksheets, and Strategies for Learning

Lauren Brukner and Lauren Liebstein Singer

Illustrated by John Smisson

£25 | $35 | PB | 216PP | ISBN 978 1 78592 761 4 | eISBN 978 1 78450 623 0

Packed with photocopiable lesson plans and tried-and-tested strategies, this illustrated guide is the ideal companion for teachers and therapists wishing to help kindergarten and elementary school children to self-regulate. It contains everything you need to integrate the successful, research-based 'Awesome and In Control' program, which focuses on empowering children to regulate their own emotions and senses and helps them to develop excellent coping strategies.

Explaining how the popular, universal 'Awesome and In Control' program works, the guide enables you to help children to keep calm and in control during everyday tasks including reading, writing and paying attention to others.

Lauren Brukner is a senior occupational therapist. She specializes in sensory integration and self-regulation strategies for children and young people, and their implementation in home, school and community settings.

Lauren Liebstein Singer is a speech-language pathologist and a licensed Teacher of Students with Speech and Language Difficulties, currently working for the New York City Department of Education.

Can I tell you about Sensory Processing Difficulties?

A guide for friends, family and professionals

Sue Allen

Illustrated by Mike Medaglia

£8.99 | $14.95 | PB | 56PP | ISBN 978 1 84905 640 3 | eISBN 978 1 78450 137 2

Meet Harry – a young boy with sensory processing difficulties. Harry invites readers to learn about why he finds it hard to process sensory information effectively, and how even simple things such as washing, dressing and coping with mealtimes can be challenging for him. He also talks about difficulties he faces at school and why large groups and loud noises are especially hard. He explains how other people can have different sensory processing issues and talks about what he and those around him can do to help.

This illustrated book is ideally suited for readers aged 7 and upwards and occupational therapists, teachers, parents, family members and friends of those with sensory processing difficulties.

Sue Allen qualified as an occupational therapist from the Welsh School of Occupational Therapy and completed her MSc with the University of Ulster. She is an experienced clinician, clinical researcher and postgraduate lecturer with a focus on families and children dealing with sensory and motor challenges. Sue was Chairman of the Sensory Integration Network from 2007 to 2013 – a not-for-profit organization that promotes education and research in sensory integration. She now lives and works in Singapore.

Stay Cool and In Control with the Keep-Calm Guru

Wise Ways for Children to Regulate their Emotions and Sense

Lauren Brukner

Illustrated by Apsley

£13.99 | $21.95 | HB | 136PP | ISBN 978 1 78592 714 0 | eISBN 978 1 78450 300 0

Meet the Keep-Calm Guru, our expert guide to the art of staying cool, calm and in control in the face of overpowering feelings!

This illustrated book introduces wise ways for children to recognize and cope with anxiety, anger, frustration and other difficult emotions. Using everything from yoga poses and pressure holds, to deep breathing and relaxing colouring activities, the Keep-Calm Guru shows kids how to take back control and feel cool, calm and just right.

Suitable for children with sensory and emotional regulation difficulties aged approximately 7–14 years.

Lauren Brukner is a senior occupational therapist. She specializes in sensory integration and self-regulation strategies for children and young people, and their implementation in home, school and community settings.

Living Sensationally
Understanding Your Sense
Dr Winnie Dunn

£13.99 | $22.95 | PB | 216PP | ISBN 978 1 84310 915 0 | eISBN 978 1 84642 733 6

How do you feel when you bite into a pear...wear a feather boa...stand in a noisy auditorium...or look for a friend in a crowd?

Living Sensationally explains how people's individual sensory patterns affect the way we react to everything that happens to us throughout the day. Some people will adore the grainy texture of a pear, while others will shudder at the idea of this texture in their mouths. Touching a feather boa will be fun and luxurious to some and others will bristle at the idea of all those feathers brushing on their skin. Noisy, busy environments will energize some people, and will overwhelm others.

The author identifies four major sensory types: Seekers; Bystanders; Avoiders and Sensors. Readers can use the questionnaire to find their own patterns and the patterns of those around them, and can benefit from practical sensory ideas for individuals, families and businesses.

Dr Winnie Dunn is Professor and Chair of the Department of Occupational Therapy Education at the University of Kansas Medical Center. She is the leading authority and internationally recognized for her research about how people respond to sensory experiences in their everyday lives. Dr Dunn has published widely and her work on sensory processing includes development of a set of measures, called the Sensory Profiles, which are used by many disciplines internationally. She lives with her husband Tim in Kansas City, Missouri.